THE LAST SUMMER OF THE DUCHESSES

Alan Castle

ATKINSON
PUBLICATIONS LTD

ABOVE: With semaphore signalling still so very much in evidence at this major railway junction, during the early months of 1964, No 46250 'City of Lichfield' approaches Platform 4 at Preston station with 3L09, the daily 10-20 Crewe to Carlisle parcels working ... a regular duty of the class in its latter years.
[Picture: Paul Claxton]

This book is dedicated to the memory of ardent enthusiast, talented photographer and lifetime friend, Paul Claxton, (1946-2009). A companion on so many adventures during the days of steam and much missed today by those who shared with him in his passions and experiences - the 'Duchesses' were undoubtedly Paul's favourite class of locomotive.

1964 - The Last Summer of the Duchesses

First published August 2014

Atkinson Publications Limited, PO Box 688, Preston, PR3 8AX
www.atkinsonspublications.co.uk

British Library Cataloguing in Publication Data.
A catalogue record for this book is available from the British Library.

ISBN 978-1-909134-11-9

Printed and bound by B&D Print Services Ltd. Marathon Place, Moss Side Industrial Estate, Leyland, Lancashire PR26 7QN

LEFT: With a load considerably less than normally found behind the tender of a Class 8P pacific, on 25th June 1964 No 46238 'City of Carlisle' passes Skew Bridge signalbox with 3K16, the 08-15 Carlisle to Crewe parcels and empty stock working. Seen one mile south of Preston, this is the point at which the four tracks of the West Coast main line diverge into six, to provide independent access for freight traffic into the Ribble Sidings and North Union yards. In its heyday, the lengthy cutting hereabouts proved to be a veritable mecca for countless generations of train-spotters and during peak periods it was quite possible to see steam-hauled excursion traffic occupying all six tracks.

RIGHT: Seemingly equally well out of place on mere goods workings, but which provided much of the 'bread & butter' work for the class in the final months of their life, No 46251 'City of Nottingham' - its LMS-style maroon livery still pristine from working a railtour to Swindon of ten days previously - pauses at Ribble Sidings on 19th May 1964 with the 4L41, 10-55 Oxley Sidings to Carlisle fully-fitted freight. Having been re-crewed here, the road to the north for the Preston crew beckons towards the notorious ascents of Grayrigg and Shap.
[Both pictures: Bill Ashcroft]

"Nothing can quite replace the majesty of a big express engine, with its spectacular appearance, its graceful action, its impressive voice and its near-human characteristics". (Cecil J Allen - 1961)

It is now exactly 50 years since the occurrence of that harrowing episode that came to absolutely overwhelm those who had grown up to know and love the atmosphere of the West Coast Main Line during the era of steam; for the closing Saturday of September 1964 transpired to be the final occasion upon which a 'Princess Coronation' pacific would haul a train in regular BR service.

A much-revered class of 38 locomotives, the 'Duchesses' - as they later became fondly known (despite 22 of them actually being named after *cities* served by the LMS Railway) - had been the enduring mainstay of motive power for principal expresses for well over a quarter of a century and, with the withdrawal en-bloc earlier that month of 15 out of the 16 survivors, the imposing Stanier predominance of the erstwhile 'Premier Line', both figuratively and literally, had just had its heart ripped out!

The enthusiast fraternity were devastated; but even absolute die-hards had been forced to accept that steam had to go one day … but, surely, not so hurriedly and with such a disgraceful lack of gratitude?

The indecent haste with which most of the erstwhile top-link 'Princess Coronation' fleet - and, of course, the many other workhorses that had served our railways for so long - came to be so-rapidly disposed of was a sad reflection upon the state of our emerging society, and the official view seemed to be that steam was the creation of a more primitive age and, quite simply, deserved no place in what was felt to be an upcoming era of new technology.

Certainly, for those who did take the time

to cogitate upon such matters, there was a sadness felt that reflected an acceptance that the life as we knew it at the time was changing; with dieselisation and electrification, perhaps for the better, perhaps not, but definitely with a realisation that changes were inevitable and counted as *'progress'*. That progress, in aspiring to get everybody and everything ever more quickly from A to B, was soon to backfire, as the so-called *'new technology'* - when it finally arrived - very quickly proved to be nowhere near as reliable and useful as anticipated. But, more upon that later …..

A Noble New Flagship for the 1930s LMS Fleet
Way back in July 1937, to mark the crowning of King George VI and Queen Elizabeth I, if not also to steal some of the thunder from the

LNER, (which had been commanding the headlines by breaking records with its own new A4 pacifics), the LMSR introduced the *'Coronation Scot'* service of streamlined trains between Euston and Glasgow. To haul these, William Stanier, the company's Chief Mechanical Engineer (or, more correctly, his chief draughtsman, Tommy Coleman), had produced detail designs for a class of 4-6-2 express passenger locomotive, appropriately to be called the *'Princess Coronation'* type.

This turned out to be a larger and more powerful development of the equally successful *'Princess Royal'* series of 13 pacifics introduced four years earlier and, in fact, the chassis of its forbearer came to be adapted to carry a larger firebox with a bigger grate area and a wider boiler-barrel with increased super-heating volume. The immediate visual impact was that this vastly improved boiler design had been mounted

much higher to accommodate all of the aforementioned features, with the front corners of the Belpaire firebox being right up to the limit of the loading-gauge and just, but only just, enabling 6ft 9in driving wheels to be accommodated underneath.

Add to that impressive equation 4 cylinders of 16½ inch diameter x 28 inch stroke, streamlined steam-passages and an immense 40,000lbf of tractive effort, all of this permitted the new engines to regularly handle trains of up to 16 coaches with ease and with tenders holding 10 tons of coal and 4,000 gallons of water - replenished from water troughs laid-down throughout the whole length of the WCML – also enabled the 401-mile London to Glasgow journey to be completed without a change of motive power en-route. A further unusual feature of *'Coronation'* Class tenders was that they were fitted with steam-operated coal-pushers to

ABOVE: *A favourite location for photographers almost since steam first penetrated the Westmorland hills, taking on board a more than ample supply of water, No 46241 'City of Edinburgh' thunders through the Lune Gorge and over Dillicar troughs with IM37, the 10-10am Aberdeen to London Euston express.* [Picture: Paul Claxton]

LEFT: *Making an unassisted ascent of the 1 in 75 to Shap Summit, on 1st August 1964, No 46257 'City of Salford' slogs past Scout Green with the 11-coaches of 1S60, the 11-40 Birmingham to Glasgow relief – a train composed entirely of ex-LMS stock.* [Picture: Bill Ashcroft]

thrust the coal towards the firing-plate. This was a unique innovation on Britain's railways and, when in operation, bursts of steam could be seen and heard rising from the rear face of the coal bunker. Such equipment greatly helped firemen to meet the high demands for power, especially during the ensuing regular non-stop runs of 299 miles that occurred between Euston and Carlisle.

If Nigel Gresley's A4 class had been considered the ultimate development of the steam locomotive in terms of maximum speed, then Stanier's own masterpiece marked a British pinnacle in terms of power output, for during tests with a 600-ton train, a drawbar horsepower of 2,511 came to be recorded - or a derived figure of no less than 3,333 horsepower at the cylinders.

De-streamlining, but post-nationalisation top-link work continues to abound

In respect of the 24 streamlined examples, a variety of problems - especially so with drifting smoke - soon started to manifest themselves. Undeniably the original *'Coronation'* pacifics had never been conceived to be as aerodynamically efficient as their East Coast rivals; the design of the 'streamlining' being construed as more of a publicity exercise than as an energy-saving feature. The consensus eventually arrived at was that this was of little value at speeds below 90 mph and the bulbous (and, arguably, not particularly attractive) extra sheet metalwork - weighing almost an additional 3 tons - was, in any case, becoming hugely unpopular with running shed personnel. Concerns had arisen as a consequence of serious difficulties encountered in obtaining access for maintenance and thus, from 1945 onwards, the casing started to be removed from those examples so-fitted. In actual fact, as the LMS era drew to a close, only three locomotives came to remain in such a state.

With duties always basically centred upon the West Coast main line itself; essentially on the heavier express turns between London Euston and Scotland, as well as services to Birmingham, Liverpool, Holyhead and, occasionally, Shrewsbury, the depots to receive allocations of the type were Camden, Crewe North, Liverpool Edge Hill, Carlisle Upperby and Glasgow Polmadie.

As regards route availability, the class was also known to have worked through to Liverpool Exchange via Preston on the occasional express from Glasgow/Edinburgh, but, due to their size and weight, they had been officially barred from the Hellifield to Blackburn, Fylde Coast, Cumbrian Coast and Windermere routes, as well as that into Manchester Victoria via Bolton.

(As a passing matter of interest, in 1953, just one *'Duchess'*, No 46241, is known for certain to have slipped through the net to work a special to Blackpool North and another was observed on the 10-00 Blackpool Central to Euston in the mid-1950s!)

Furthermore, despite *'Duchesses'* appearing on occasional trains into Manchester (London Road) from the south, no turntable in that immediate locality was large enough to accommodate their 73ft 10¼ in length and any such visitors had to run light all the way out to Stockport to turn on the closest available triangle.

In Scotland, on ex-Caledonian tracks they were regular performers over Beattock as far north as Perth, Glasgow (Central) and Edinburgh (Princes St), as well as also making quite frequent appearances over the Glasgow & South Western main-line into Glasgow (St Enoch).

Undoubtedly, few British expresses have had a more varied history than the LMSR's *'Midday Scot'*. Inaugurated in 1891, the afternoon service between Euston, Edinburgh and Glasgow became the first Anglo-Scottish train composed entirely of corridor stock. By 1936, the 'down' train comprised of never less than 14 vehicles, amounting to at least 445 tons, which demanded haulage throughout by one of the Stanier Pacifics over the 401 miles without change between Euston and Glasgow. This came to be one of the most exacting schedules in

LMSR history, but one that was well within the capabilities of these fine machines and such tasks became one of the major components of their 'bread & butter' employment.

The 'Semis', as they had become known to generations of trainspotters in post-war years, turned the heads of bystanders wherever they appeared. Certainly, well into the late 1950s and early 1960s, for the train-watcher lucky enough to have been standing at the south end of Preston station on any day of the week at around 1-40pm, given that the working timetable indicated that it should occur, when such *did* happen there was no finer sight than to be confronted with two immaculate pacifics approaching each other, each bearing a tartan headboard, roof-boards and tail-end gangway cover proclaiming it to be the 'up' or the 'down' *'Royal Scot'* express.

Sadly, such extravagances as locomotive headboards and carriage destination boards began to disappear nationwide during the Sixties, and most of the titled trains were then named only in the timetables, becoming otherwise totally anonymous. Express steam power was also very much on the wane.

1955 Modernisation Plan for British Railways portends great changes afoot

Throughout the 1940s and 1950s, whilst other European and American countries were actively experimenting with - and rapidly introducing - diesel and electric technologies, UK railways remained suffused in the tradition of steam. Diesel-engine traction development had, for many years, been ensconced in lower-power shunter types and undoubtedly it wasn't until a pair of Co-Co prototypes - built to explore a use for

LEFT: During the early 1960s, and at a time when trespassing didn't appear to be of such a major issue as it became in later years, whole families used to flock to the huge cutting that extended southwards from Preston, intent upon a day's picnicking combined with a little trainspotting. Here, at Farington Curve Junction, (more locally known as Bee Lane), the 1L27 reporting number on the transparently obvious centre of attraction - No 46240 'City of Coventry' - confirms that this is the up 'Lakes Express' - notably composed, on this occasion, entirely of ex-LMS stock. [Picture: Bill Ashcroft]

RIGHT: An unusual elevated view of the northern exit to Preston station - as seen from County Hall on 28th May 1964. To detach a few vehicles conveying traffic for the Preston area, No 46238 'City of Carlisle' pulls out from under Fishergate bridge whilst shunting the stock of 3L14, the afternoon Crewe - Carlisle parcels. Metrovick Co-Bo diesel D5705 (now preserved) waits in a siding, ready to pilot the down 'Lakes Express', which will eventually precede 3L14 northwards. [Picture: Bill Ashcroft]

larger locomotives - were ordered by the LMS from English Electric and delivered in 1948, that matters started to change.

Nos 10000 and 10001 were 1600hp diesel-electric designs aimed primarily at passenger services. Both ran until the mid-1960s and much of their design did eventually come to provide the basis for several later classes of production locomotive, including the English Electric Type 4s. The later Nos 10201 & 10202 were 1,750hp 1-Co-Co-1 models based on 10000 and 10001, being produced for the Southern Region between 1949 and 1953 and, as successful designs of more powerful traction-motors began to evolve, a 2000hp No 10203 also entered service in 1954. The SR trio were eventually transferred to the LMR in 1954/5 and it was now inevitable that they were soon to appear at the head of former *'Duchess'* workings, including the fabled *'Royal Scot'*.

Notwithstanding such pioneering developments, there had been a period in the immediate post-war years during which attempts

were made to construct modern and more reliable steam as the way forward for the then newly-nationalised railway system, rather than to leap headlong into untried and untested dieselisation. There were also political, as well as practical, reasons behind any resistance to change. In essence, whilst still recovering from the consequences of the War, the Labour Government of Clement Attlee did not want to significantly reduce the demand for domestically-produced coal in favour of imported oil, for this could well have affected the nation's balance of payments and, potentially, might also have created much unemployment. Despite this, a *'Modernisation Plan'* report came to be published by the British Transport Commission in January 1955, essentially the intention being to elevate the UK railway system into the 20th Century – and as a matter of urgency!

Key aspects included electrification of principal main-lines (such as those from London to Birmingham, Liverpool and Manchester) and

large-scale dieselisation elsewhere to replace steam. Correspondingly, despite the ambitious earlier aspirations of the BTC design teams, many new classes of steam locomotive that did manage to see the light of day ultimately came to be sent for scrap well before their 10th birthdays. Some were hardly 'run-in' and, clearly, no matter in what way such an unfortunate situation was perceived, it was all a shocking and disgraceful waste!

For all that, despite the beginning of the end for all steam power now clearly being in sight, visions of more modern traction never came to inspire as much as their majestic, living, breathing predecessors. Ugly shapeless boxes exuding foul exhausts, the latter were devoid of any character whatsoever and, wherever one now looked, never again were platform ends to be crowded with the hordes of excited train-spotters that such erstwhile *'meccas'* once enjoyed!

With hindsight ... the folly of interim dieselisation

It soon came to be realised that a 2,000hp machine, being closely equivalent to the likes of a Class 7 *'Britannia'* steam locomotive, did not really meet the most onerous requirements of the heavy, fast trains previously handled with ease by the Stanier pacifics and, consequently, failures were becoming ever more common-place. When a steam loco was in trouble, it could generally struggle home, but when a diesel sat down on the main-line, it totally stopped the job!

LEFT: During the early summer of 1964, No 46225 'Duchess of Gloucester' departs from the south end of Preston station with 2K82 the 06-20 Carlisle to Crewe all-stations 'stopper'. Often a duty for a pacific and for a Crewe North top link crew working home, the 'parliamentary service' – as it would have been known in earlier days - will make nine further calls before Crewe is reached. The footbridge above the leading coach is the erstwhile "Glass Bridge", that formerly provided direct access to the L&Y/ LNW Joint 'Park Hotel' – by this time relegated to use merely as county council office accommodation. [Picture: Bill Ashcroft]

RIGHT: On the damp summer Saturday morning of 15th August 1964, a fairly pristine maroon No 46245 'City of London' stands under the ex-Caledonian gantry at the south end of Carstairs station with 1M32, the Saturdays only 11-50 Glasgow Central – Morecambe, which it worked as far as Carlisle. Very evident in this view is the recently-applied yellow cab-side stripe that indicated that, after 1st September, the loco was not to be permitted to work under overhead electrified lines south of Crewe. A rather academic exercise, it might be argued, as the class was to be withdrawn en-bloc a mere fortnight after that date! The large collection of corridor gangway covers is equally clear enough indication of the importance of this junction as the combining point of portions of expresses from Glasgow and Edinburgh that were to head south across the border into England. [Picture: Dick Manton]

Nevertheless, the dieselisation programme continued unabated and contracts quite noticeably came to be awarded primarily to British suppliers ... perhaps just because they were British. Be that as it may, as mentioned above, with little opportunity to provide for a still steam-acclimatised home market, the majority very quickly turned out to possess limited experience in diesel-locomotive manufacture and the subsequent rushed commissioning, based on an expectation of rapid electrification, resulted in generally poor designs, that were also accompanied by a total lack of standardisation or compatibility. As in other areas, this had the knock-on effect of causing the retention of steam on the West Coast main-line for considerably longer than had been anticipated.

That Robert Riddles had frequently argued the case in the early 1950s for embodiment of a Standard Class 8 Pacific into the standard range of locomotives being introduced by British Railways - and the eventual birth of 71000 *'Duke of Gloucester'*, accompanied by its

inherent subsequent poor steaming characteristics and heavy fuel-consumption - are aspects already too well-documented to be repeated here. Likewise, equally well-acknowledged is how a series of errors perpetrated by *'The Duke's'* builders only really came to be rectified when preservation beckoned and, following which, the opportunity was taken to incorporate some other improvements that totally transformed the performance of a design that could otherwise have become a hugely successful and cost-saving new class for its original progenitors.

We must also reflect upon the fact that, at late 1950s / early 1960s prices, to construct further 8P class locomotives would probably have cost about a quarter of the cost of equivalent diesels ... motive power that was, in any case, generally meant only to be a stop-gap measure until full-electrification arrived. Even based on an assumption that, because of the better availability of diesels, twice as many steam locomotives would have been needed, this still meant that the capital cost of a fleet

Total electrification finally manifests itself

25kV electrification had been proceeding up the WCML towards the capital for some years and, due to restricted clearances through some tunnels and bridges, many of which would have been prohibitively expensive to rebuild, the overhead catenary on several of the later-energised sections had to be installed at a lower height than was standard elsewhere (specifically to accommodate a reduced 13ft 1in loading-gauge, instead of the more normal 13ft 6ins).

This meant that, being higher from rail-level than was thought to be practically safe, as from 1st Sept 1964, several steam classes, including the 'Royal Scots', 'Patriots', 'Jubilees', Fowler 4Fs, ex-LNW 7Fs and 'Coronation' Pacifics, were officially excluded from travelling under the wires anywhere south of Crewe. Indeed, for some time previously, yellow diagonal stripes had started to be painted on the cab-sides of many locomotives that might have been expected to otherwise venture out of Crewe in that direction. With Type 4 haulage now predominant

elsewhere on London Midland Region main lines anyway, although their coal-pushing tenders had been valued in overhead electrified areas as an insurance against footplatemen attempting to climb into tenders to trim coal forward, little suitable work could now be found for the still very much serviceable 8P Pacifics.

Effectively, such an edict pronounced the beginning of the end for the 'Coronations', for a major portion of their 'raison d'être' was now being denied to them. In fact, commencing at the end of 1962, with the introduction of more modern (but not necessarily as powerful or even anywhere near as reliable) traction, several of the class - including all of the eight Scottish Region examples - had already been withdrawn. On the other hand, many of the English contingent continued in service for a couple more years; in point of fact continuing to regularly work across the border, but by this time generally on much less prestigious duties.

1964 dawned with several of the class survivors in store, but, to satisfy seasonal requirements, gradually the majority of these were eventually

of diesels would have been about twice that of an equivalent fleet of the latter.

Power-wise, confirmation that a 'Duchess' was virtually a match for a 'Deltic' (at that stage, the most powerful type in service) was afforded through the 1955 series of tests conducted with a member of the class on the Settle & Carlisle line. This was of interest insofar as it demonstrated that the power-output of such a locomotive was constrained merely by the rate at which a fireman could shovel coal into the firebox. Whereas those test results were achieved through the utilisation of two firemen, it seemed to have been the case that a properly-developed BR Standard 8P would not have been so similarly restricted!

At any rate, as regards spending money on improving steam performance until such time as full-scale electrification could have taken over, it would definitely have been intriguing to discover the effects of such a rebuild upon any of the existing larger British locomotives of the period and, in particular, of the already successful 'Princess Coronation' design. Undeniably there had been proposals in LMS days to develop a 'Super Coronation' with an even greater-size firebox, that would have pushed the wheel arrangement up to a 4-6-4, but quite probably due to the Second World War, this design never made it beyond the drawing board.

Had there been a case for the class to remain in service beyond 1964, the potential would clearly also have been there for rebuilding along the lines of those improvements made to an example of the South African Railway's Class 25NC, perhaps with under-feed stoker, gas-producer firebox and modified draughting. Unquestionably, following its rebuilding by English engineer, David Wardale, into the solitary Class 26, tests revealed a measured increase in equivalent drawbar power of 43%, this being accompanied by a 28% reduction in coal and water consumption. Applying the same figures to the 'Duchesses', in performance terms this might have produced something potentially quite phenomenal!

returned to traffic. On 15th June - at the commencement of that year's summer timetable – with over half of the class having already gone, a considerable amount of good work was still being performed by the remainder, and this often still being on top-link duties.

All of that was soon to come to an end, however, come the day that some anonymous accountant in his ivory tower at 222 Marylebone Road decided that the 8Ps were superfluous to requirements and issued the infamous mandate to the depots that the class were to be withdrawn en-bloc as from the week ending 13th September.

The 1964 Summer Timetable

Of the 19 examples ostensibly still in traffic as at 15th June, only 46226 'Duchess of Norfolk' appears not to have turned a wheel during the whole of the period. Although it remained in a steamable condition and was believed to be otherwise mechanically sound, the 12A Kingmoor loco was side-lined at Upperby depot, reportedly with cracked frames and awaiting repair. Those repairs were never undertaken.

The rest of the fleet soldiered on - and very much hard at it until the bitter end – often also on exceptionally heavy trains that were already proving to be a challenge to their invariably under-powered diesel replacements!

With so much of the latter-day work transpiring to take place during the hours of darkness, a survey recently undertaken to collate all the surviving records of duties from which the following notes are extracted, is, at best, random and, given the still vast extent of the 'Princess Coronation' sphere of activities, the approaching 800 currently-known sightings are probably no more than a tip of the proverbial iceberg. Nevertheless, one factor that does appear to stand out is that, despite what senior management had decreed, the 8Ps appeared to be far too valuable to the operating departments to lose and the latter were clearly intent upon hanging on to them for as long as possible …

indeed with one or two being observed still hard at work days after being officially condemned!

The paragraphs that follow, therefore, are intended merely as an illustration of the sort of tasks upon which those 18 active engines were engaged during their final weeks and, given that the full list of sightings has been condensed from reports provided by well over 100 separate observers, obviously no guarantee can be provided as to absolute accuracy.

46225 'Duchess of Gloucester' (12B) (Maroon)

This Carlisle engine had been particularly busy throughout June and into July 1964, especially on journeys back and forth over Shap; these interspersed with a single trip to Holyhead and a couple more as far north as Perth. On 4th July, it made its only known visit to the London area, being seen heading a morning express passenger towards Euston. Spending three days on Willesden MPD, it returned north on 7th July with 4Z61 13-55 Willesden-Carlisle special fitted-goods. On 16th July,

proceeding northwards from Crewe, it was seen taking over 1S81 13-35 Euston-Perth, returning the following day at the head of 1M46 21-00 Glasgow (Central)-Marylebone postal – the latter duty which it worked on at least a further two occasions during the ensuing fortnight. Proceeding overnight Crewe to Perth on 31st July with 1S03, the 19-20 ex-Euston, it returned the following afternoon to Carlisle with 1M37, the 12-coach 10-17 Aberdeen-Euston.

Notwithstanding such undeniably onerous tasks, 46225's crowning glory was yet to come, for, on 12th August, it was rostered for the crack Glasgow-Euston 'Caledonian' express – presumably replacing a failed Type 4 diesel. Following this outstanding honour, a lowlier task ensued, for it was provided at Perth the following afternoon to work 3M04 the 14-15 Aberdeen-Manchester (Oldham Rd) express fish back to Carlisle.

Perhaps then entering a period on a depot 'stand-by' basis, it disappeared for around a week before commencing its final round of duties. On the 20th it appeared on 3K13 04-28 Carlisle-Crewe parcels and was next seen on the 22nd, (taking over at Penrith from a smaller

loco that had worked to that point via Keswick) with 1K76 08-20 Workington-Crewe. It then sojourned on Crewe North shed for a few days before making the final journey of all on 26th Aug at the head of 3L14 13-40 Crewe-Carlisle parcels. The following day, *'Duchess of Gloucester'* was observed dead on Upperby shed – its career apparently now well and truly over.

46228 'Duchess of Rutland' (5A) (Maroon)

No 46228 was another very active engine, putting in very frequent appearances at Euston, Glasgow, Perth, Llandudno and Holyhead. Kicking-off the summer timetable on 17th June, with 3L09 10-20 Crewe-Carlisle parcels, it returned to base very early the following morning with 4K00 04-54 Carlisle-Crewe fast goods. Crewe North very smartly turned it round the same day to take over 1S81 13-25 Euston-Perth, which it appears to have worked only as far as Carlisle, for on 19th June it was seen arriving at Liverpool (Lime St) at the head of 1M18 23-30 from Glasgow. Spending the next night on Edge Hill shed, the latter also soon found a task for it; the pacific being observed passing Crewe - running around an hour late - at the head of the 14-10 Liverpool (Lime St)-Euston and clearly substituting for a failed AC electric.

The month of July was spent entirely shuttling between Crewe and Carlisle/Glasgow, and mainly on Anglo-Scottish passenger turns, before making its first appearance of the summer in the London area on 4th Aug with 3A34, the 17-vehicle 12-00 Holyhead-Willesden parcels ECS. Resting overnight on Willesden depot, it was soon appropriated to work north again with 4M93, the 23-wagon 18-10 Chatham-Stockport (Adswood) fitted-freight. This was only the start of a busy few days, which then saw *'Duchess of Rutland'* heading expresses to/from Carlisle, Perth, Holyhead and Llandudno. Its final appearance in Euston station came on the evening of 3rd Sept, when it was seen arriving with an *'Irish Mail'* relief, 1A44, the 12-coach 16-00 ex-Holyhead.

LEFT: The road is clear on the down-fast line as No 46225 'Duchess of Gloucester' passes Euxton Junction on 30th June 1964 with 3L14, the 13-40 Crewe to Carlisle parcels. A particularly heavy load on this date, several of the vehicles will probably be shunted from the train during its scheduled one-hour call at Preston. The tracks diverging to the left are the former L&Y lines via Bolton to Manchester Victoria. [Picture: Bill Ashcroft]

RIGHT: 46228 'Duchess of Rutland' departs southwards from Preston over the River Ribble bridge on 15th May 1964 with 3K16, the 08-15 Carlisle to Crewe parcels and empty stock train. Colloquially known to generations of railwaymen as "The Horse & Carriage", this regular Class 7P or 8P duty could by no means be described as an express duty, having already taken 5 hours to cover the 90 miles between Carlisle and Preston and with lengthy wayside calls still to make both at Wigan and Warrington. [Picture: Bill Ashcroft]

On 8th Sept, after spending a couple of days on Kingmoor shed, it was sent back to its home base via 4K00 04-54 Carlisle-Crewe freight and was promptly returned back north on 3L14 13-40 Crewe-Carlisle parcels. On Friday 11th Sept, it worked south again with 3K16 08-15 Carlisle-Crewe parcels and, once more, Crewe was equally rapid in turning it around to take out a northbound relief (which was probably 1S77 15-40 (FO) Crewe-Glasgow – a regular *'Duchess'* duty at the time); being observed on Polmadie depot on 13th Sept. It was not seen at all the following day at Crewe North shed and where all of its other, by now withdrawn, sisters had been placed into store, so 46228's final journey south therefore still remains a mystery, but which was quite probably overnight and, apart from the exploits of No 46256 recounted later in the book, could very well also have constituted the final working of all of the entire class.

46235 'City of Birmingham' (5A) (Green)

No 46235 commenced the summer timetable by being provided by Crewe North on 19th June to take over 3X20, a Cardiff to Perth pigeon special as far as Carlisle; following which it was sent back south on the *'Northern Irishman'*, 22-00 Stranraer-Euston. Several other overnight sleeper turns followed and 46235 was another of its type that saw much use at the London end of the WCML until the 1st Sept steam ban came into effect; for example, being observed on 1st July taking the 11-coach up *'Lakes Express'* southwards from Crewe and, yet again, on 25th July with 1A85, a relief to the above train. Unusually, throughout the entire period under review and although once a fairly commonplace occurrence, this was the only class member that seems to have penetrated through to Shrewsbury; being seen on shed there on 18th July.

Back over Shap on 1st Aug with 1S26 23-40 Euston-Glasgow, this was the start of a week of working expresses over that section, before being seen on 10th Aug heading south with 3K16, the legendary 08-15 Carlisle-Crewe parcels … a train colloquially known to generations of railwaymen and enthusiasts as *"The Horse & Carriage"* and a favourite turn for the class in their latter years.

On 15th Aug, 46235 headed south from Crewe once more with 1A35 12-25 Blackpool (Central)-Euston, and yet again on 22nd Aug with 1A25 09-05 Llandudno-Euston. Unfortunately, on the latter occasion, the pacific had only got as far as Rugby before it ran a hot-box and had to be taken off its train; subsequently being noted on Rugby shed at around 15-00hrs.

One week later, the problem seemed to have been satisfactorily rectified for, on 28th Aug, it passed through Carlisle heading-up 1S03 19-20 Euston-Oban/Perth. On this particular date, the train had been loaded to 17 or possibly 18 bogies including sleepers (of around 600 tons) and proceeded to climb unassisted over Shap. The train was checked just short of the summit and then restarted without a trace of a slip, to clear the top at 18 mph! As one of its passengers observed, the tape-recording that he obtained *'was something else'* - especially with the sound of the coal-pusher working flat out, *"sounding like the crack of a whip, seemingly urging the locomotive on"*!

Witnessed on 1st Sept at Crewe, working a Euston-Holyhead service, two days after that it was back in Perth to take over 1M37, the 12-vehicle 10-10 Aberdeen-Euston. It appears to have been taken off at Carlisle and then to have resided on Upperby shed for a couple of days, before running light back to Crewe on 5th Sept and where restoration for preservation beckoned. *'City of Birmingham'* was eventually dispatched from Crewe Works adorned in the superb BR lined-green paintwork that it still carries today and the locomotive is currently on static display in the city after which it was named. Hopefully, one day it will be permitted to work again … and, in so-doing, to provide a fine figurehead for the municipality that came to be its saviour.

LEFT: *Shap Summit - 916 ft above sea level and highest point on the West Coast main line between Euston and Carlisle – sees No 46235 'City of Birmingham' racing south past the loops that still exist here today with 1M25, the 10-15 Glasgow Central to London Euston. [Picture: Arthur Haymes]*

RIGHT: *Whilst many freight workings at the time operated on a weekdays-only basis, the then still very lucrative parcels traffic continued to be a 7-day operation. Here, on the sunny Sunday morning of 30th August 1964 and in a scene totally transformed today (other than the LMS coaling plant which continues to dominate the skyline over the town – albeit no longer in use), No 46237 'City of Bristol' displays some serious steam leakage as it heads away from Carnforth with 3L09, the 10-20 Crewe-Carlisle parcels. [Picture: Peter Fitton]*

As an aside, another preserved class member, withdrawn in the February, was seen travelling up the West Coast main line on 14th Sept 1964 and, coincidentally, on the same day that appears to have been the very last normal service working of any of its sisters. Running as train 6Z02 Crewe to Heads-of-Ayr, (4)6233 *'Duchess of Sutherland'* was hauled dead over Shap behind Black Five 45026, with another of the same class taking it onwards from Carlisle. Amongst several other ex-BR locos, this particular example was one of three LMS pacifics that had been purchased by entrepreneur Billy Butlin to place on static display at his holiday camps. No 6233 was to remain at the Heads-of-Ayr camp until Feb 1971, following which all of the Butlin's exhibits gradually came to be passed to preservationists for restoration to working order.

46237 'City of Bristol' (12B) (Green)

'City of Bristol' was another well-travelled Upperby loco that reached Euston - and even Holyhead - on at least one occasion during the period under review, but got to Perth three times and, otherwise, came to spend the majority its summer generally shuttling between Carlisle and Crewe on a mixture of express passenger, parcels and fully-fitted goods turns.

It commenced in fine style on 15th June, working through from Perth to Crewe with 1M12, the 21-00 to Euston. On the 24th, it brought 1M23 10-10 Edinburgh (Princes St)-Birmingham into Crewe and was sent back the following day on 3L07 22-50 Willesden-Carlisle parcels. A similar pattern ensued daily until 20th July, when it was seen at Euston preparing to take out 1D41 08-05 Euston-Holyhead - which it headed as far as Crewe, before then being sent north to Carlisle with that same evening's 3S07 18-50 Crewe-Glasgow (Central) parcels.

Four days later, on 24th July at Carlisle, 46237 took over 1M17 the 23-45 Edinburgh (Princes St)-Birmingham (New St), but got no further than Clifton & Lowther - where it failed - and sister Upperby loco 46250 had to be hurriedly dispatched from Carlisle to replace it. Presumably the cause of the failure was nothing serious, for on the 29th, it had reached Crewe and where it was seen taking over 4L41 10-55 Oxley-Carlisle fully-fitted goods.

LEFT: *Fully-fitted goods workings became a staple part of the Stanier pacifics' diet during their final years. On 24th June 1964, a commendably clean No 46238 'City of Carlisle' slowly by-passes the platforms along the down through road at Preston with 4L41, the 10:55 Oxley to Carlisle. These tracks are truncated today, being a far cry from the immediate post-war years when Preston was sorely stretched at busiest periods such as the "Wakes Weeks", with workers from many industrial towns flocking to the coast in their droves and necessitating excursion traffic having to utilise these otherwise goods-only lines. [Picture: Bill Ashcroft]*

BELOW: *On a beautifully sunny, if somewhat hazy, day in late spring 1964, No 46237 'City of Bristol' rolls into Lancaster (Castle) station with 1S51, the 09-25 Crewe-Perth. The main buildings here date from 1902, being styled on mock-Elizabethan lines, clearly with the intention of mirroring the battlements of the nearby Lancaster Castle. [Picture: Paul Claxton]*

On 12th Aug, having worked from Perth as far as Carlisle with 3M04 18-44 Aberdeen-Manchester (Oldham Rd) express fish, it retired to Upperby shed and where it seems to have remained for a good fortnight, possibly under repair once more, before being seen again on 28th Aug heading south on the *'Northern Irishman'* 1M14 22-00 Stranraer-Euston. Crewe North shed immediately appropriated it the same day to work another Irish boat train, this time to Holyhead, with 1D41, the 08-05 ex-Euston.

On 31st Aug, 46237 was back on familiar ground, working over Shap and Beattock with 1S61 11-20 Birmingham-Glasgow, returning the following morning with 1M24 10-05 Glasgow-Birmingham … trains that both invariably loaded up to 16-bogie formations. Clearly, the loco seemed to be still experiencing problems, for its next reported sighting was not for another week, when it was seen passing Boars Head Jct on 8th Sept with an unidentified working. On 12th Sept, it was rostered for 1A33 08-40 Carlisle-Euston, returning from Crewe to its home depot that night on what was thought to have been 1S03, the 14-coach 19-20

Euston-Perth.

Well after the 12th Sept deadline set for withdrawal of all surviving class members, there are strong indications that, on 14th Sept, 46237 was seen heading a northbound parcels between Crewe and Carlisle and, if true, that would almost certainly have been 3L09 10-20 Crewe-Carlisle parcels (a regular Class 6, 7 or 8P duty in 1964). Apart from the special duties assigned for 46256 (as detailed below … or possibly despite our uncertainty surrounding 46228, as above), 46237 would appear to have been the very last of any of the class to have worked a train whilst still in BR service.

46238 'City of Carlisle' (12B) (Maroon)

The undeniable star celebrity of Upperby depot, *'City of Carlisle'*, started its own summer on 15th June, running light from Edge Hill shed to head 4L26, the 19-00 St Helens-Carlisle freight. A couple of days later it headed south again on passenger duty at the head of the up *'Northern Irishman'*, returning once more on an Oxley-Carlisle class 4 freight – a task which it undertook a further three times over the course of the following few weeks. On 27th June, it appeared at Carlisle station to take over 1X78, which was, presumably, a Euston-Glasgow extra and, on 4th July, made its only appearance at the southern end of the WCML with 1M34, a seasonal relief from Glasgow to Euston. Three days later, it was back in Carlisle, to take southwards 3K13 04-28 parcels to Crewe, returning on 10th July with 4L40 02-05 Oxley-Carlisle fully-fitted goods.

For reasons that remain unclear, 46238 then disappeared into its home depot for 24 days, only reappearing on 3rd Aug to work 3K13 again, returning north on 6th Aug with 3L09 10-20 Crewe-Carlisle parcels. On 15th Aug, it was seen heading up no fewer than 15-bogies on 1L25 10-30 Euston-Carlisle & Windermere. Several trips to Perth followed, including the 1A99 12-05 Perth-Euston relief as far as Crewe on 15th August, but its crowning glory was yet to come. Having gone south on an evening freight turn on 3rd Sept, the following day it was rostered to work the last-ever steam-hauled *'Caledonian'* express, from Crewe to Carlisle. Whether or not this was to cover for a failed diesel - or even someone's eminently admirable idea of a swansong for the class - will probably never now be known.

Its final tour of duty probably commenced on 8th Sept, when it was seen at the head of 3K16 08-15 Carlisle-Crewe parcels. The return working north has gone undocumented, but, following which, 46238 was withdrawn immediately upon its return to Upperby shed.

46239 'City of Chester' (1A to w/e 29/08/64, then to 5A) (Green)

Nothing was heard of this engine for a good two weeks into the summer timetable and then, all of a sudden, it materialised on the up *'Lakes Express'*, running from Crewe to Euston, on 30th June. Returning to Crewe with freight, 46239 was then returned to the London area on a parcels turn, before retiring to Willesden shed for a further eleven days. Whatever had ailed the loco – if, in fact, anything had – it appeared to

have been rectified by 16th July, for 46239 then appeared in Euston to work 1D82, an evening *'Irish Mail'* relief to Holyhead. Following that, it made several trips to Glasgow on night sleeper expresses and 1M24 10-05 Glasgow-Birmingham as far as Crewe on the 24th, then back over to Holyhead once more, before retiring to Crewe North depot for a couple of days. On 29th July, no less than the up *'Royal Scot'* saw *'City of Chester'* working it out of Euston as far as Crewe. Continuing on such top-link work, the following day 46239 took over the up *'Lakes Express'* at Crewe, heading back into Euston.

The loco then 'disappeared off the radar' for yet a further three weeks, possibly surplus to requirements - given that steam was rapidly receding at its then Willesden home - before appearing yet again on the up *'Lakes'* on 21st Aug. Early the following morning, it was sent north on 1D41, another relief to Holyhead, but was later seen heading back south on 1A46 10-53 ex-Workington – this running 8 hours late and quite obviously as the result of another steam substitution for diesel.

Having worked more *'Irish Mail'* reliefs, and now transferred to Crewe North, 46239 was next seen on 3rd Sept arriving at Perth on 1S25 22-50 ex-Euston. Perth sent it out again, as far as Carlisle, with 3M04 18-44 Aberdeen to Manchester fish train. The following morning, it continued further south on 3K16 the 08-15 Carlisle to Crewe "Horse & Carriage" parcels. As mentioned earlier, a train that quite regularly saw the big pacifics in their final days, 3K16 regularly took very nearly five hours to reach Preston from Carlisle, so this could by no means have been considered an 'express' duty!

Into its final week of service and on 7th Sept, *'City of Chester'* took 1L25 10-30 Euston-Carlisle northwards from Crewe, returning the

following day on 4A08 12-50 Carlisle to London (Broad St) meat and milk train, before appearing again at Perth on the 11th to head up 3M04 once more. Three days later, it was seen back at its home shed ... and, in line with instructions received from 'up above', was now withdrawn from service.

46240 'City of Coventry'
(1A to w/e 29/08/64, then to 5A) (Maroon)

Curiously, until the infamous steam ban south of Crewe came into force, this popular red pacific seems to have spent its first ten weeks of the summer timetable engaged entirely on duties south of Crewe. It started the period on 19th June with the first of a couple of passenger jobs into Euston, namely on 1A46, the 10-53 ex-Workington. On 22nd June it worked the 18-10 Euston-Liverpool and two days later was seen at Bletchley on a northbound working of *'presflo'* cement wagons.

On 11th July, it appeared in its namesake city, prepared to work a holiday special bound for Eastbourne. Presumably, once it had reached the London area, 46240 came to be exchanged for doubtless

inferior motive power from that point onwards to the south coast! A series of parcels and relief workings came next, the climax of which being at the head of the relief *'Irish Mail'* of 2nd Aug and upon which a couple of enthusiasts had managed to secure a footplate ride from Crewe southwards. A photograph does exist of the locomotive speedometer reading 98mph between Lichfield and Tamworth!

Three further Euston-Crewe trips then occurred on the down *'Lakes Express'*, before *'City of Coventry'* finally condescended to head northwards out of Crewe once more; appearing over the border in Perth on 29th Aug with 1S81 13-35 Euston-Perth, before being sent back to Carlisle the following day with 1M12 21-50 Perth-Euston. Paucity in information at this point suggests that 46240 may well have disappeared into Upperby depot until 5th Sept, at which point it headed south with 1G14 08-20 Carlisle-Birmingham. Its final duties of all have gone unrecorded, being last witnessed on 7th September, heading north through Wigan with an unidentified fitted freight and then being seen on Kingmoor shed the following afternoon.

LEFT: *With safety valves feathering, on Saturday 25th July 1964, a none-too-clean No 46241 'City of Edinburgh' exits the Lune Gorge and leans to the super-elevated curves that proliferate in this locality, as it hurtles past Grayrigg signal box and commences the long descent to the Lancashire plain. The reporting number 1M26 indicates that the train is the 09-00 Perth to London Euston - a service which this Stanier pacific will work from Carlisle to Crewe. [Picture: Peter Fitton]*

ABOVE: *A very last journey before withdrawal and, given the original work specification for the 'Duchesses' such as that depicted in the previous picture of this same locomotive, being engaged upon a task that brought a somewhat ignominious end to a distinguished career. On the evening of 4th September 1964, No 46241 departs southwards out of North Union Yard at Preston and heads past the adjoining Ribble Sidings with 6P12, the 18-10 freight to Warrington. From Warrington, it would run light its home depot of Edge Hill. [Picture: Peter Fitton]*

46241 'City of Edinburgh' (8A) (Green)

Commencing the summer timetable heading a couple of fitted-freight turns between Carlisle and Edge Hill, 46241 nevertheless found its way into the London area by 20th June with 1A46 10-53 Workington-Euston. Back on freight once more - both north and south of Crewe - it soon re-appeared on top-link duties, on 8th July at Crewe, taking over 1L25 10-30 Euston-Carlisle, closely followed a couple of days later by 1S77 15-40 (FO) Crewe-Glasgow. The very next day, it was appropriated by Upperby for 1M32 11-50 (SO) Glasgow-Morecambe and which 46241 took through to its destination … a very rare occurrence indeed! Retiring for the weekend to Carnforth shed, it was sent out early on the Monday morning with 5F07, the 03-25 freight departure that was to get it back to its Edge Hill home once more.

A week then seems to have passed by before more top-link employment beckoned and when a departure from Crewe was observed with 1A46 yet again. Returning north immediately with overnight trips, it had reached Polmadie by the 22nd, and 25th July

found it heading south on 1M26 09-00 Perth-Euston. Back on Crewe-Carlisle parcels jobs (such as 3L09 and 3L14) for 4 or 5 days, by the 31st 46241 had returned to passenger duty with 1M47 21-00 (FO) Glasgow-Euston and was next seen on 6th Aug on 1A99, which was a Carlisle-Euston extra. Several freight jobs and an overnight Perth-Euston relief over Shap immediately followed, before 46241 finally found itself at Kingmoor shed on 25th Aug, destined to end its career with 15 days engaged entirely upon freight work.

Spending the next 4 days heading 4F08 16-55 Carlisle-Edge Hill and its return, 4L26 19-00 St Helens-Carlisle, the 30th of the month saw it on 4A08 12-50 Carlisle-Broad Street express meat and milk, to Crewe. The following day witnessed the engine being sent light over to Warrington to work out the remainder of the week on 6P12 08-37 Warrington-Preston NU yard and 18-10 return. For local enthusiasts, this provided the very unusual sight – especially at such a late date - of a Stanier pacific being serviced on Lostock Hall shed! The last glimpse of *'City of Edinburgh'* was a week after this, back at its home depot, but by now very much withdrawn from service.

LEFT: *Posing between the more usual 2-8-0s to be found at Carnforth MPD, an exceptionally unusual sight of a pair of Edge Hill pacifics together presented itself on Sunday 12th July 1964. No 46241 'City of Edinburgh' had been appropriated by Upperby shed to work 1M32, the 11-50 Glasgow (Central)-Morecambe (Promenade) seasonal extra and which it worked throughout to its destination. Retiring for the weekend to Carnforth shed, it was sent out early on the Monday morning with a freight duty that got it back to its home depot.*
No 46243 'City of Lancaster', meanwhile, had arrived after working a train of cement 'Presflos' to the yard at nearby Bay Horse, in connection with the construction of the new M6 motorway northwards from Preston. Reporting number 5X05 indicates that it is about to depart with the return working to Snodland (Kent). No 46243 would appear on this particular working on at least 7 separate occasions during the 1964 summer timetable. [Picture: Peter Fitton]

RIGHT: *Out in the open country on the Preston to Lancaster 'racing stretch', working a turn that quite regularly saw Stanier pacifics in their final years of service, but provided little chance for high-speed running, a less than pristine Edge Hill example, No 46243 'City of Lancaster', heads north near Brock water troughs on 15th July 1964 with 4L41, the 10-55 Oxley (Wolverhampton) – Carlisle fully-fitted freight. The booked return working southwards was overnight on a Carlisle – Edge Hill Class 4 freight. [Picture: Bill Ashcroft]*

46243 'City of Lancaster' (8A) (Maroon)

Being observed on Day 1 of the summer timetable passing Rugby working 1M11, the 22-45 Glasgow-Euston 'Night Limited', 46243 was immediately dispatched back to its home depot at the head of 1F26 12-20 Euston-Liverpool (Lime St) – a duty which it worked throughout. Nearly 3 following weeks seem to have transpired with no recorded sight of 'City of Lancaster', before it eventually re-appeared on 5th July, when it was seen heading for Crewe on the 10-10 Liverpool-Euston and then being almost immediately dispatched further south the very same afternoon with 1A46 10-53 Workington-Euston.

After this, commenced what appeared to be over a month of non-passenger duties, including 3 consecutive days hauling cement 'presflos' on 5X40 02-30 Willesden-Bay Horse and 5X05 17-50 Bay Horse-Snodland - these being special workings conveying materials to site for the construction of the new M6 motorway northwards of Preston. Having worked 3L14 13-40 Crewe-Carlisle parcels on 12th Aug, the following day it found itself rostered onto 2K82 06-20 Carlisle-Crewe all stations 'stopper' … the so-called 'Parliamentary' of former days. This was often a duty for a pacific and for a Crewe North top-link

crew working home. The following night it re-assumed top-link status, taking 1S03 19-20 Euston-Perth, through from Crewe to Perth and then returning on 1M12, the 21-50 to Euston as far as Carlisle. Seemingly afterwards having returned to Perth on a similar duty, it departed south for home from Carlisle on the 24th with 4F08 16-55 Carlisle-Edge Hill.

Edge Hill depot, however, clearly had no immediate need for it on the 'home-front' at this time, for the pacific was sent back north with the following evening's 4L26 19-00 St Helens-Carlisle. 46243 then spent 6 days shuttling back and forth over Shap between Carlisle and Crewe, mainly with parcels trains and expresses to/from Glasgow and Edinburgh. Arriving in Princes Street on 1st Sept with 1S62, the 11-30 from Birmingham and returning the following morning with 1M23, the 10-10 departure back to Birmingham, this was the last ever occasion when a 'Duchess' was to appear at the Scottish capital … at least in normal service.

Making its final southbound run over Shap on 7th Sept with 7G02 05-08 Carlisle-Bushbury, the end was clearly nigh and 46243 spent the next 3 days back on the Snodland to Bay Horse cement trains, before being returned to Edge Hill once more and where it was finally withdrawn from service.

46244 'King George VI' (12A) (Maroon)

This loco brought the 1M11 'Night Limited' of 15th June from Glasgow as far as Crewe and from whence, as mentioned previously, sister 46243 then took over. Arriving back in Glasgow 6 days later, 46244 was sent south on 1V41 21-25 to Kensington Olympia and it then seems to have retired to Kingmoor depot for a couple of weeks, before surfacing at Perth once more on 11th July. Many more jobs followed, essentially between Glasgow and Carlisle and usually on passenger turns, the most notable of which being on the 22nd, when it was seen taking 1M46, the 19-00 mails to Marylebone out of Glasgow (Central), incongruously being piloted on this occasion by Type 1 diesel D8113!

By 1st August, 'King George VI' had penetrated through to Crewe with the previous evening's 1M46 19-00 Glasgow-Marylebone, and was immediately dispatched back north with 1S42 00-10 Euston-Glasgow Central, through to Glasgow. On the 8th it was back once more, heading the 09-15 ex-Liverpool Exchange and returning south yet again with 1M46. Nothing is recorded for the following 7 days, but 46244 turned up again on 16th August working Crewe to Carlisle with the down 'Midday Scot' – a regular steam turn throughout the summer on Sundays only.

LEFT: No 46244 'King George VI' climbs the bank out of Preston station, with 4L41, the 10-55 Oxley to Carlisle fitted freight on 4th August 1964. The huge ex-LNW Preston No 4 signalbox, seen behind the loco, opened in 1902 and was, for many years, the longest on the LNWR system, eventually coming to possess 184 levers. Following the commissioning of the new Preston power 'box, it was demolished in 1973. [Picture: Bill Ashcroft]

RIGHT: On Sunday 15th August 1964, a commendably clean No 46245 'City of London' passes Broughton (north of Preston) on the up fast line with 3A08, the 13-00 Carlisle to Broad Street combined express meat and milk train. Although a regular steam duty, Stanier pacifics only appeared on this working on five occasions during the 1964 summer timetable. [Picture: Peter Fitton]

In Perth on the 20th for the 3M04 18-44 Aberdeen-Manchester fish, it next appeared yet one more time in Glasgow on the 22nd with 1S44, the seasonal 08-50 relief from Blackpool Central.

Following a boiler wash-out at Kingmoor, on the 30th it was seen on 1M18, the 23-30 to Liverpool (Lime St) – a working which it took, via Wigan, right through to its destination. A few days later, on 2nd Sept, it was back in Perth to take over 3M04 again. Yet a further 2 days after this, it made a further appearance on 3M04 and on the 11th it headed 1S53 09-25 Crewe-Perth throughout, before appearing that night yet one more time on 3M04!

On 12th Sept, 46244 would make its final visit to Perth, by means of 1S53. Returning south under cover of darkness on 1M12 21-50 Perth-Euston, it arrived at Carlisle during the early hours of 14th Sept, whereupon it retired to Kingmoor shed for withdrawal.

46245 'City of London'
(1A to w/e 25/07/64, then to 5A) (Maroon)

Being another Willesden loco and by this time with few duties to undertake, 46245 didn't seem to have done very much until 4th July, when it was seen passing Watford on 1A46 10-53 Workington-Euston. But much more frequent employment was to follow (particularly on this very same duty), until on the 15th when it was seen leading 1A34, the up 'Lakes Express' into the capital. On the 24th it then made the first of only two known trips north of the border - all the way from Crewe to Perth - on 1S03 19-20 Euston-Perth/Oban, returning to Crewe the following evening with 1M15 18-00 Inverness-Euston sleeper.

Following the working of a couple of pilgrimage party-specials southwards from Coventry and Liverpool, on 8th Aug a particularly busy day involved taking in 1L27 11-40 Euston-Workington 'Lakes Express' as far as Crewe, making a quick visit to Crewe North shed and then continuing north at the head of 1L35 18-37 Crewe-Carlisle. Apparently then taking a breather for 6 days, another very active period commenced on 14th Aug, when 'City of London' was seen heading up 1S77 15-40 (FO) Crewe-Glasgow throughout. The following morning, it was dispatched back to Carlisle with 1M32 11-50 (SO) Glasgow-Morecambe and, on the 16th continued southwards back home to Crewe with 3A08 13-00 Carlisle to Broad Street express milk. Having taken 1S03 19-02 Euston-Inverness as far as Crewe on 21st Aug, it then seems to have retired into North shed's roundhouse for several days of 'fettling-up' before being dispatched over to Derby to participate in the Works Open Day.

Being, by now, in pristine external condition - and with the requested 46256 being unavailable - on 1st Sept it became prime candidate to work an 'Ian Allan' Paddington-Crewe-Paddington enthusiasts' railtour. Following this brief intrusion into alien Great Western territory, with the ban south of Crewe now in place, 46245 disappeared for 7 days, eventually materialising again on 8th Sept at the head of 1S53 09-25 Crewe-Perth. Upon arrival at Carlisle, it was immediately turned round to head back to Crewe with 1M23 10-10 Edinburgh (Princes St)-Birmingham (New St).

The final tour of duty saw 46245 departing Carlisle on the 11th with 4A11 16-18 freight to Willesden. Coming off at Crewe, it was sent back north the following morning with 3L09 10-20 parcels to Carlisle and, with withdrawal of the whole class now being effective, Upperby immediately sent it back home to Crewe North on the 13th with its final trip of all, 7G02 05-08 Carlisle-Bushbury goods.

46248 'City of Leeds' (5A) (Maroon)

'City of Leeds' commenced the summer timetable bringing 1M14 22-00 Stranraer-Euston into Crewe on 16th July, and then entered into almost 3 weeks of journeying entirely south of that point on a variety of parcels and fitted goods turns. On the 22nd, it appeared in Euston to head the otherwise now regularly diesel-hauled *'Merseyside Express'*, which it proceeded to take merely as far as Nuneaton. Perhaps this was the point where this diagram normally changed from Type 4 diesel to 25kv electric power, but whatever the case, 46248 was seen later that day heading light to Rugby before returning light again back to Nuneaton, via Coventry … presumably utilising such an itinerary as a means to turn. The following day it was particularly active, first of all taking 1M14, the overnight from Stranraer, back into Euston and then working 1S06, the evening Stranraer boat train, back as far as Crewe.

Appearances were then a little sporadic, or at least until 25th July, when it appeared on the North Wales coast on expresses between Crewe and Holyhead and, on the 27th and 29th it departed from Euston on evening Holyhead extras that it worked throughout. 46248 also reached Carlisle, when on both 18th July and 1st Aug it was seen departing for Crewe with 1G14 08-20 Carlisle-Birmingham. It then even reached as far north as Perth, arriving on 13th Aug with 1S07 19-40 sleeper from Euston.

Its next sighting was passing through Preston the following morning with 4V65 07-36 Carlisle-Cardiff fitted goods, being seen the following night heading back towards the border city with 1S82 19-10 Euston-Inverness. Upon arrival there, it was immediately turned round and sent to Penrith to work 1K76 08-20 Workington-Crewe.

Interspersed only with 1S07 19-40 Euston-Perth sleeper on the 21st, almost a fortnight of mainly parcels and fitted goods turns south of Crewe saw 46248 enter into its final few days of life, and of shuttling

entirely between Crewe and Carlisle. On 28th Aug, it worked 1A33 08-42 Carlisle-Euston, heading north again that night with 1S03, the 14-coach 19-20 Euston-Perth and back home the following morning with 1G14 once more. There is an unconfirmed report of it being seen at Wigan on 31st Aug, of which no further detail is available and it was, in any case, seen withdrawn on Crewe North shed very shortly afterwards.

46250 'City of Lichfield' (12B) (Green)

One of the busier members of the class during the period under review, *'City of Lichfield'* kicked-off on the 14th, 15th and 16th June heading, respectively, 3L09, 3K16 and 3L14 parcels (details above) and then on 19th June it appeared on 1M46 19-00 Glasgow-Marylebone postal. However, it only got as far as Carnforth on the latter before it had to be removed with a failed LH injector. This soon being fixed by the fitters at Carnforth depot, a couple of days later it was back in traffic, being employed once more on precisely the same diagrams as previously.

26th June was a particularly hectic day, commencing with 2K82 06-20 Carlisle-Crewe 'stopper' and returning northwards that night all the way to Perth with 1S03 19-20 (FO) Euston-Perth/Oban. On 4th July, it was down in London departing for Crewe with the *'Lakes Express'*, before then being immediately sent forward with 3L19 18-37 Crewe-Carlisle parcels. 46250 must then have reached the Liverpool area on an overnight passenger (probably 1M18), for, on 7th July, it worked 4L26 19-00 St Helens-Carlisle fast goods, returning immediately on 4F08 02-16 Carlisle-Edge Hill. Following this were a few days of mainly top-link passenger turns, these including the regular Sundays only *'Duchess'* working on the down *'Midday Scot'* of 19th July.

On 24th July, it was sent out light from Upperby to Clifton & Lowther (just south of Penrith) to relieve sister 46237 – which had failed on 1M17, 23-45 Edinburgh (Princes St)-Birmingham, departing from this point 71 mins late. It was sent back north the following day with 1S97, an 11-30 Birmingham to Glasgow relief.

On 29th July, its crowning glory occurred when 46250 worked the up *'Royal Scot'* from Carlisle to Crewe, after D313 had failed and was seen the following day back on Upperby shed. Its final and even more hectic week in traffic commenced on 2nd Sept, in working 1L25 10-30

LEFT: The evening 'rush hour' has commenced at Preston and a Stanier predominance in motive power is well in evidence. No 46250 'City of Lichfield' is already running at around 15 minutes after its booked time as it prepares to depart Platform 5 with 1S81, the 13-35 Euston - Perth. Alongside, in Platform 4, No 45606 'Falkland Islands' is drawing slowly towards the water column and will soon follow northwards with 1L32, the 17-22 Manchester Victoria - Windermere commuter 'residential'.
[Picture: Peter Fitton]

RIGHT: With a head at every single droplight and most other windows as well, the performance of No 46251 'City of Nottingham' is certainly the centre of attention as it surmounts the summit of Grayrigg bank on 12th July 1964 with the SLS Birmingham to Carlisle "Pennine Pacific" railtour. The climb now momentarily over, the fireman has put on the injector in preparation for the slog to come over Shap Fell.
[Picture: Peter Fitton]

Euston-Carlisle, 1M26 09-00 Perth-Euston on the 3rd, 1S77 15-40 (FO) Crewe-Glasgow on the 4th, 1M46 19-00 Glasgow(Central)-Marylebone mails on the 5th, 1M18 23-30 Glasgow-Liverpool (Lime St) on the 6th, heading back north with 4L26 19-00 St Helens-Carlisle goods on the 7th.

On 9th Sept, it had reached Crewe for the final time, and when it took out 1S81 13-05 Euston-Perth. As no records appear to survive to suggest that the loco took the train through to Perth (this more generally being the case) it must be assumed that 46250 was removed at Carlisle. That tour of duty successfully accomplished, it is then believed to have been placed in store at Kingmoor depot – never to work again.

46251 'City of Nottingham' (5A) (Maroon)

'City of Nottingham' was to become another latterly to be distinguished loco that saw much use on passenger work to Glasgow, Perth, Holyhead and Euston. Being seen on 16th June on a Crewe-Holyhead-Crewe diagram, it then retired onto Crewe North shed to be 'bulled up' to work a LCGB railtour on 21st June from Coleham Jct (Shrewsbury) to Paddington via Birmingham (Snow Hill). South of Bicester, a maximum speed was recorded of 93mph and, from Paddington the next day, 46251 seems to have run light to Rugby shed and where its supreme external condition had decreed it the ideal candidate to become standby loco for a Royal Train working.

Ultimately, such services not being required, it was returned north to Crewe the following day with a parcels train and then remained at Crewe North shed for a further 10 days or so, before re-appearing on 5th July to take northwards the down 'Midday Scot'.

Very active the following week, on 12th July, it worked throughout from Birmingham New St to Carlisle with the SLS 'Pennine Pacific' railtour and, in fact, handing over to sister 46255 at Carlisle. During the following two months, 46251 was a particularly active member of 5A's allocation - appearing generally at the head of express passenger turns, these interspersed with the occasional parcels job - at Glasgow, Perth, Carlisle, Liverpool, Morecambe and Euston. It then disappeared for yet a further fortnight, before being turned out for its final tour of duty of all, in appearing on 12th Sept on 3L09 10-25 Crewe-Carlisle parcels, being rostered by Upperby the following morning to head 7G02 05-08 Carlisle-Bushbury back as far as Crewe.

46254 'City of Stoke-on-Trent' (5A) (Maroon)

This was yet another of the hard-working Crewe North stud that started off its summer on a veritable miscellany of express passenger, parcels, fitted-freight, milk, fish and even petrol-tanker workings and, in the process, reaching such destinations as Perth, Glasgow, Carlisle, Holyhead, St Helens, Edge Hill and Euston.

On 4th July, 46254 departed Glasgow at the head of 1M35, the 13-15 to Euston, returning from Crewe to Carlisle the next afternoon with the down 'Midday Scot'. The following day, it found itself on 1A69 16-30 Carlisle-Willesden express milk train, but on 8th July, whilst working 4F08 16-55 Carlisle-Bushbury fitted, it failed at Preston and had to repair to Lostock Hall MPD for attention.

This, clearly, was a problem that seemed to have been rectified fairly promptly, for two days afterwards, it was observed heading out of Carlisle again with 4A08 12-50 Carlisle-Broad Street express meat

and milk train. Following that brief spurt of activity, it didn't seem to have shown its face outside of Crewe roundhouse for a full 3 weeks to follow, with its next sighting not being until 1st Aug when it was seen heading north with 1S97 12-52 Euston-Glasgow relief. The next day, it departed Carlisle with 1M22, the up 'Royal Scot', a duty which it may very well have worked throughout. Then followed a couple of trips to Holyhead and yet a further two more to Perth, before returning to home base during the early hours of 15th Aug with 1V42 22-00 Glasgow-Kensington Olympia sleeper.

The subsequent fortnight seems to have found 46254 under repair or, at very least, merely on standby duties, for it was not until 30th Aug that it surfaced again, heading north out of Crewe with the down 'Midday

Scot' and this would appear to have been the final occasion upon which any 'Duchess' was to work a titled express. Yet a further day to the fore, and on 31st Aug it then headed its final observed passenger turn of all, on 1S25 22-50 Euston-Perth northwards from Crewe, returning to Carlisle with 3M04, Aberdeen-Manchester fish.

'City of Stoke-on-Trent' was, however, seen back on Perth shed the following day, having arrived on an unidentified duty. After this date, only two isolated workings were noted; namely on 5th Sept with 4A11 16-18 Carlisle-Willesden freight (loaded to a massive 50 wagons) and then on 12th Sept, with 3L14 13-40 Crewe-Carlisle parcels. Although not actually being observed - and no date being recorded, the final duty of all, to get it back to its home depot, would probably have been 1M46 19-00 Glasgow-Marylebone mails.

46255 'City of Hereford' (12A) (Green)

It was a whole week into the summer timetable before this Kingmoor pacific appeared off-shed, when it worked 1S07 22-50 (SO) Euston-Inverness sleeper from Carlisle to Perth, returning to base with that evening's 1M12 21-50 Perth-Euston. Then performing a couple of jobs

to Glasgow and back, it retreated back into the depths of Kingmoor shed for yet another week, presumably to be cleaned and otherwise prepared to work the SLS 'Pennine Pacific' railtour of 12th July between Carlisle and Leeds. Two days after this, it was noted on Edinburgh Dalry Road depot, being readied to take out 1M23 10-10 Edinburgh-Birmingham as far as Crewe.

Similar sojourns south of Carlisle occurred on the 28th and 29th July, when it was seen both days on 1M24, the regular 13/14-coach 10-05 Glasgow-Birmingham. Following a few days of working out of Perth and Glasgow, it materialised at Crewe again on 11th Aug, to take over 1S81 13-05 Euston-Perth, hauling this through to its destination.

Perth became 46255's favoured venue for the last few days of its career, working through from Carlisle on 2nd Sept with 1S53 09-25 Crewe-Perth and back to Carlisle the following evening at the head of 3M04 18-44 Aberdeen-Manchester fish. Having reached Perth once more, (quite possibly on 1S25 22-50 Euston-Perth, northwards from Carlisle), it completed its final tour of duty on 13th Sept with 3M04 18-44 Aberdeen-Manchester (Oldham Rd) fish, taking this as far as Carlisle and from whence it retired to Kingmoor shed.

PREVIOUS PAGES - LEFT: *On 1st August 1964, threatening skies loom over a classic Lune Gorge location – one today totally destroyed thanks to the hugely intrusive presence of the M6 motorway. The fireman of No 46254 'City of Stoke-on-Trent' is evidently preparing for the assault upon Shap Fell with 1S97, a Euston to Glasgow Central relief – a train particularly pleasing upon the eye in that it is composed entirely of 11 ex-LMS vehicles, even a such a late date. [Picture: Peter Fitton]*

PREVIOUS PAGES - RIGHT: *Having just passed underneath the former Midland line to Settle Jct and with the long-closed original MR motive power depot building clearly visible in the right background, on 2nd August 1964, No 46254 'City of Stoke-on-Trent' approaches Carnforth with the up 'Royal Scot'. This is a historic picture that really did mark the end of an era, as it transpired to have been taken on the last ever occasion when this prestigious express was destined to be hauled by a Stanier pacific. [Picture: Peter Fitton]*

LEFT: *In the sort of inclement conditions for which the Settle & Carlisle line is renowned, No 46255 'City of Hereford' approaches Ais Gill summit on 12th July 1964 with the SLS 'Pennine Pacific' railtour, a special that had arrived in Carlisle off the West Coast main line behind sister No 46251 'City of Nottingham'. No 46255 had taken over to work the train between Carlisle and Leeds. [Picture: Bill Ashcroft]*

BELOW: *A commendably clean No 46256 'Sir William A Stanier FRS' takes on water in the now long-vanished down mainline platform at Carnforth on 2nd September 1964, during its scheduled call there with 3L09, the 10-20 Crewe-Carlisle parcels. To the right can be seen the LMS coaling plant, which still survives today – albeit no longer used. The signals in the foreground are 'banner repeaters' that merely indicate the state of the mandatory signals situated out of sight underneath the over-bridge and at the far end of the platform. [Picture: Paul Claxton]*

46256 'Sir William A Stanier FRS' (5A) (Maroon)

From the start of the summer timetable, for nearly a whole month, the celebrated Ivatt pacific was employed essentially on heavy parcels and fast fitted-goods turns. For example, on 19th June, it was seen heading up 46 wagons with 4S69 16-18 Camden to Glasgow (Sighthill) and on 1st July, when it worked a 17-vehicle 3A34 12-00 Holyhead-Willesden empty parcels. The latter train being once again observed on 28th Aug with the same loco, this time it was even heavier laden to an incredible 20 bogies – a task that might have proved somewhat daunting for a mere EE Type 4!

Having reached Perth twice on passenger jobs - on 7th and 18th July - 46256 had gravitated to North Wales by the 25th, when it was seen heading 1P05, a Llandudno to Preston relief. Taking the ECS onwards to Morecambe, the next day it was noted as far south as Camden on 4S68, a 46-wagon fitted-freight heading for Glasgow (Sighthill), before then vanishing for a few days, only re-appearing on the 31st, departing Crewe for Perth with 1S25, the 22-50 ex-Euston.

Upon arrival, 63A dispatched it immediately back to Carlisle with 1M37, the 13-coach 10-10 Aberdeen-Euston and the next morning it was seen heading south again from Penrith with 1K76 08-20 Workington-Crewe. Within 48 hours, it was in Perth yet one more time to make the first of two additional appearances within 4 days. A Class 2 stopping-passenger service followed on 9th Aug, when it was seen on 2P84, the regularly steam-worked 16-30 Carlisle-Preston, after which it ran light to Crewe.

A relatively quiet week then ensued, it being seen on merely a couple of 'Irish Mail' reliefs to/from Euston. Conversely, the following period proved to be particularly hectic for 'Sir William', for, on four consecutive days commencing 18th Aug, it worked 3L09 10-20 Crewe-Carlisle parcels, 3K16 Carlisle-Crewe parcels, a Crewe to London area 49-wagon fitted-freight (piloted by 'Black Five' 45434), 3A34, a 20-vehicle Crewe-London parcels and 1A31 06-38 Workington-Euston. On the 25th, it took 1A43 10-43 Windermere-Euston southwards from Crewe, before disappearing for 8 days until 2nd Sept when it departed Crewe once more with 3L07 21-53 Willesden-Carlisle parcels. Returning home the following day under cover of darkness, 3L07 had been its final observed duty before the official withdrawal date of the other class survivors.

However, following the intervention of senior management, it was granted a temporary reprieve for another couple of weeks and to ensure that it remained in full working order, 46256 continued to appear on a few workings. The first of these found it at Carlisle on 10th Sept to head 1A33, the 08-40 Carlisle-Euston. Having presumably arrived on an overnight duty, it was next seen at Polmadie shed on 14th Sept before heading back south that same evening on 1M46, the 19-00 Glasgow Central to London Marylebone – presumably as far as Crewe. On 16th Sept it headed north once again at the head of 1S53 09-25 Crewe-Perth, returning as far as

LEFT: No 46257 'City of Salford' hurtles down the 1 in 75 of Shap Fell and past the tiny isolated level-crossing signalbox at Scout Green on 15th August 1964 with the 10-10 Edinburgh Princes St to Birmingham express. This train was worked by steam on only five occasions throughout the whole of the 1964 summer timetable, hence taking the photographer completely by surprise. [Picture: Peter Fitton]

RIGHT: The last of the line and the final development of the fleet, No 46257 'City of Salford' - the only BR-built Stanier/Ivatt pacific - passes under Skew Bridge and approaches Farington Curve Junction with the 18-coach combined Workington and Perth to London Euston. Unusually, it is seen on this occasion utilising the up-slow line and probably running slightly late, thus keeping out of the way of a Blackpool Central to Manchester Victoria DMU already halted in the up fast line platform at Leyland and which would be turning left at Euxton Junction. [Picture: Bill Ashcroft]

Carlisle that same evening with 3M04 18-44 Aberdeen-Manchester (Oldham Rd) fish. The very next afternoon, it continued to home base with 4A11 16-11 Carlisle-Willesden fitted-freight. The following 9 days were spent inside Crewe North shed being prepared for the swansong of the class – the RCTS special of 26th September.

46257 'City of Salford' (12A) (Green)

Commencing the summer with a couple of jobs south of Carlisle that included 3K13 04-28 Carlisle-Crewe parcels on 18th June, 'City of Salford' was then to spend almost a fortnight of being entirely engaged upon workings to/from Glasgow and Perth and mainly on overnight expresses. The spell was broken on 31st July, when it worked from Glasgow through to Crewe with 1V84, the 19-15 to Plymouth, with Crewe then sending it back on 1S60, the 11-coach 11-40 Birmingham-Glasgow relief. After 6 days of resting on Kingmoor shed, 46257 worked north to Perth once more with 1S53 09-25 Crewe-Aberdeen, coming home that night with 3M04 18-44 Aberdeen-Manchester fish.

Appearing next on Polmadie shed, by 10th Aug it was back in Crewe to work 1S53 as far as Carlisle and on the 15th it took 1M23 10-10 Edinburgh (Princes St)-Birmingham through to Crewe. Three days after that, it was in Perth yet one more time, to take over 1M37, the 12-coach 10-10 Aberdeen-Euston. On 25th Aug, it seems

to have worked the up 'Thames-Clyde Express' (or, at least, a relief to this) from Glasgow (St Enoch) to Carlisle, presumably deputising at this very late date for a failed 'Peak' class diesel.

Inactivity appears to have followed for around 12 days, before 46257 commenced its final tour of duty in working an unidentified express from Carlisle to Perth on 5th Sept, returning on the 5th with 1M12, the 21-50 to Euston, which it may very well have taken through to Crewe. Its very last revenue-earning movements are unrecorded, but on 11th Sept it was photographed on Wigan Springs Branch shed, being cleaned ready to run light to Manchester Victoria the following day in order to be exhibited as part of the 'British Railways Queen' event that was to take place in Victoria's Platform 11. (Incidentally, the young lady who was crowned that day was Norma Corrigan - the daughter of the Newton Heath shed-master at the time.) Immediately following the ceremony, 46257 ran light to Preston shed (reportedly via Newton Heath depot) and where it

was placed into store. On 28th November, it travelled north to join other withdrawn class members in the Upperby scrap line, being hauled dead in a freight train headed by 'Black 5' 44934.

And that appeared to be that. Albeit perhaps merely as a gesture of defiance by the depots towards those unseen and anonymous accountants, one or two Duchesses had survived for a day or two more beyond the official deadline, their ultimate destiny was inevitable.

Even though a single exception, living very much on borrowed time, was to survive for a couple of additional weeks, this was merely to honour a contractual agreement and the summer of 1964 really had witnessed the end of an era. Mere words will never adequately describe the loss felt by so many, but such anguish was destined to continue with a vengeance ... for the final demise of steam was now less than four years away!

REQUIEM TO A LEGEND
THE 'SCOTTISH LOWLANDER' SPECIAL
of 26th SEPTEMBER 1964

"There are not enough superlatives in the English language to describe a 'Princess Coronation' locomotive in full cry. We shall never see their like again". [O.S. Nock - 1983]

(26665)
British Railways Board (M)
Railways Correspondence & Travel Society
THE SCOTTISH LOWLANDER
SATURDAY, 26th SEPTEMBER, 1964
CREWE, WARRINGTON, PRESTON,
CARLISLE, HAWICK, MILLERHILL,
NEWINGTON, FALKIRK, COWLAIR.
JNC., SPRINGBURN, DUKE STREET,
GALLOWGATE, KILMARNOCK,
DUMFRIES, CARLISLE, PRESTON,
WARRINGTON, CREWE
SECOND CLASS   For conditions see over
0436

THE
RAILWAY CORRESPONDENCE
AND TRAVEL SOCIETY

60004 William Whitelaw near New Cumnock on 30th June, 1963
(From a photograph by R. A. Lissenden)

ITINERARY OF THE
SCOTTISH LOWLANDER
Saturday, 26th September, 1964

Tour organised by the Lancashire and North West Branch

RIGHT: *During its last few weeks before its protracted withdrawal from service, seen passing through the long-abandoned platforms of the former Grayrigg station and, with the Westmorland hills as a looming backcloth, No 46256 'Sir William A Stanier FRS' races south with 1K76, the 08-20 Workington and Keswick to Crewe on 1st August 1964. It will have taken charge of the train from an Ivatt 2-6-0 at Penrith, having run light from Upperby depot. [Picture: Peter Fitton]*

It was a wet and gloomy September Saturday evening exactly 50 years ago that was to witness the final occasion upon which a *'Princess Coronation'* pacific would haul a train in regular BR service. Certainly, in whatever manner one chose to view matters, that 26th September 1964 date still recalls hugely evocative memories for all those, such as this writer, who had been lucky enough to have been on board the Railway Correspondence & Travel Society's *'Scottish Lowlander'* railtour and of the occasion when those notorious gradients of the Westmorland Fells came to resound for that very last time to the deep, powerful exhaust beat of a Stanier *'Duchess'* at the head of a heavy express train.

Throughout the closing years of the steam era, Bill Ashcroft had been the secretary of the Lancs & North West Branch of the RCTS and one of a committee of 5 members (consisting of Duncan Farquhar, Dick Dyson, Noel Machell, Nobbie Clark, Ted Wright and Bill) who had been organising some extremely interesting steam-hauled railtours that had regularly been taking place throughout the North-West of England. It was during the course of 1963 that Bill and his colleagues had come to learn *'on the grapevine'* of a rumour that the London Midland Region intended to withdraw all of its remaining Stanier pacifics during the closing months of that same year and, as a result, the quite unanimous decision was very quickly arrived at to engage upon their boldest venture thus far - the *'Duchess Commemorative Railtour'*.

The main stamping-ground of the class over the historic Shap and Beattock climbs being still available to steam operation, a plan was drawn up and a proposal put to BR to operate a special train between Crewe and the soon-to-be-closed Edinburgh Princess Street terminus. The suggested itinerary being mutually agreed as viable, the tour was eventually pencilled-in for Saturday October 5th 1963.

Planned swan-song for the 'Princess Coronation' Class

As such an occasion might very well have turned out to be the ultimate 'grand finale' for the class as a whole, right from the commencement of negotiations, a further desire was expressed for the train to be headed by the eminently appropriate No 46256 *'Sir William A Stanier FRS'*. This request appeared also to have been agreed to in principle, but, sadly however, in due course a bogie defect had occurred shortly before the actual tour date, this resulting in another red example – No 46251 *'City of Nottingham'* - being offered instead. As a matter of fact, the latter was specially brought out of store by Crewe North shed for the event.

The weeks slipped by and bookings were proceeding at a fairly healthy pace, but, as the big day drew ever closer, all the indications were becoming abundantly clearer that the remaining *'Princess Coronations'* were likely to survive for just a little while longer than had originally been anticipated and, quite possibly, even well into the

following year. Naturally, this news was greeted with some relief by the enthusiast fraternity, but, come what may, such was the interest being shown that the decision was made that the tour should still go ahead.

On the actual day, much to the delight of those aboard, a well-filled rake of 11 ex-LMS vehicles came to make an unassisted ascent of Beattock Bank, and, especially on during the return leg, some exceedingly lively running took place both north and south of the border.

Despite all the odds, the class enjoys a reprieve and a repeat tour is organised

Now back in regular traffic - and perhaps due to its exemplary external condition - the following year, *'City of Nottingham'* in fact came to work a further three tours for other societies and, equally surprisingly, at the start of the 1964 summer timetable on 15th June, fourteen other members of the class were still hard at work. Very clearly, from that

point forward, with the introduction of the usual seasonal 'reliefs' and 'extras', much additional work had obviously become available and it perhaps went without saying that, with the chronic unreliability of replacement diesel motive power, the continuing availability of the Class 8Ps came to be much utilised throughout this period.

For all that, what with the impending ban on the greater part of steam's sphere of operation south of Crewe and further 'modern traction' becoming available by the day, the threatened death sentence for the big pacifics could only be temporarily delayed for so long and there was no argument that it now made sense for the RCTS to run yet another similar tour at some time during the coming autumn ... if that were at all possible.

Always ones to select combinations of highly imaginative itineraries allied to equally attractive motive power, the six Lancs & North West Branch committee members had been very conscious that main-line steam was now very much on the wane north of the border and even the fabled Waverley Route had come to be threatened with total extinction. As a result - and to offer a little variety – both the North British line from Carlisle to Edinburgh via Hawick and the Glasgow & South Western route from Glasgow to Carlisle via Kilmarnock were specifically selected to be woven into a proposed tour-schedule and the detail of this was soon being placed before the various regional operating authorities. With regards to appropriately suitable motive power for the lines concerned, the desire was expressed for a Gresley A3 pacific to be supplied to work the train over the Waverley Route, a rebuilt 'Royal Scot' or 'Patriot' for the G&SW line ... and a 'Princess Coronation' from Crewe to Carlisle and back.

LEFT: The date that the remainder of the seventeen other working survivors were to be officially withdrawn had come and gone and 'Sir William' hadn't turned a wheel since its own last outing to Carlisle of over a week and a half prior to that. In order to ensure that it remained in full working order, 46256 then came to be rostered for a few more workings, the first of which found it at Polmadie shed on 14th September – having presumably arrived there on an overnight sleeper duty. Here, in the early evening light, it is prepared to work south again with 3M10, the 23-45 parcels train from Glasgow to Crewe. [Picture: Dugald Cameron]

RIGHT: The date is now Friday, 25th September 1964 and in the depths of the roundhouse at Crewe North depot, the very last operational 'Princess Coronation' pacific, No 46256 'Sir William A Stanier FRS' is being subjected to the attentions of the shed's cleaning gang. No strangers to preparing railtour locomotives in the 1960s, work is just about complete and steam is being raised in preparation for the locomotive's final tour of duty the following day. [Picture: Bill Ashcroft]

The response was awaited, perhaps with trepidation, but Bill, however, had another card up his sleeve which he now brought into play.

At that period in time, his contact at the LMR Stoke Divisional Office was the redoubtable George Dow, who was then Divisional Manager and a lifelong enthusiast. As regards the itinerary, Mr Dow clearly must then have performed a significant role in bypassing all the inevitable red-tape that usually ensued and a satisfactory agreement was soon being concluded.

Concerns expressed by officialdom over requested selection of motive power!

Despite this achievement, George was unable to persuade the Scottish Region authorities to grant the specific locomotive requests placed before them. In respect of both the A3s and also the Stanier 7Ps, the official response had come back that *"there won't be any available in September"*. Certainly, with steam disappearing at an alarmingly rapid rate, there was no reason to believe, by that date, that such a situation would not be the case.

So, although a disappointment, this state-of-affairs was accepted philosophically ... for, after all, Mr Dow had already obtained BR's commitment to supply a 'Duchess' for the Crewe-Carlisle leg and, surely, that was all that really mattered! Furthermore, at long last - *and* as originally desired - there was every chance that the elusive No 46256 could now be utilised ... albeit always on the understanding that it would still be serviceable by that still distant date.

It might be mentioned at this juncture that the Scottish Region were also invited to produce suggestions of their own as regards suitable *alternative* motive power that *they* might find acceptable. One of the offers that came back was to provide an A4 Pacific instead ... but only *if* the Society would be prepared to pay the costs of moving it from Aberdeen Ferryhill depot to Carlisle. That additional expense was estimated to be £191, but, faced with the alternative option of two 'Black Fives', or even two 'Standard Fives', the former, very clearly, appeared to be the eminently preferable solution!

No 60007 'Sir Nigel Gresley' was the one that the RCTS felt was the most notable of the type still at work and, of course they were obviously secretly entertaining thoughts surrounding what might create a memorable engine change at Carlisle … whilst undoubtedly also wondering, *had* this highly significant pair ever been seen together before? Despite this, for their own part, in being desirous to select the most reliable of the survivors, the Scottish Region had clearly wanted such a high-profile train to be worked by the last of the class to go through works and another Ferryhill example, No 60009 'Union of South Africa' was offered.

Nevertheless, the RCTS held out in its determination to get No 60007 'Sir Nigel' and, with George Dow's further intervention and support, eventually got their own way.

However, noting the Scottish Region's apparent hesitancy, Mr Dow then pulled a master-stroke in suggesting that, as the Society were now to be paying extra for a specific type of loco, BR, for their part, should *guarantee* A4-haulage throughout and to provide an assurance of fitness of their selected motive power to complete the commission.

If even *that* much was not enough, they then went even one better in providing 'Number 9' as a standby loco and, quite amazingly, also arranged for it to be waiting, fully prepared, at Niddrie West Junction near Edinburgh. Whether, in practise, this stipulation would really have been necessary or not has gone un-recorded in the mists of time, but, in order to ensure adequate coal in the tender for the return to Carlisle – a matter that ultimately did cause some concern at the stage when the special was traversing the latter part of the Waverley Route - the train actually exchanged locos at Niddrie. So, on the day, the Society got *two* A4s for the price of one - literally!

Meanwhile, death sentence is pronounced for the remaining 'Duchesses'

The planned route for the 'Scottish Lowlander', including the avoiding of the Edinburgh Waverley bottle-neck by utilising the goods lines and the Edinburgh suburban line from Niddrie Yard and then travelling round the 'back-streets' of Glasgow from Cowlairs, through Springburn, St John's and bypassing St Enoch, onto the G&SWR. This

totalled around 545 miles of continuous running, but, amazingly, the price of a ticket for such a marathon jaunt turned out to be a mere £3.7s.6d (£3.37p) and, even with inflation, that fare today seems to have been an absolute bargain! Some 502 people had placed advance bookings, so, in view of this a 12-vehicle restaurant car train also was also promised and such dining facilities were, evidently, going to be utilised to the full!

Meanwhile, all of the pre-tour publicity had already gone ahead and bookings were starting to roll in, when rumours emanating from the 'grapevine' were now suggesting (correctly, as it transpired) that all the 'Duchesses' were to be withdrawn 'en bloc' - and irrespective of condition - on September 12th 1964.

Calamity ensued … for, clearly, this would be a full two weeks prior to the tour! Quite obviously, the accountants hadn't forgotten their earlier threats and even the requirements of a handful of railway enthusiasts were now considered highly unlikely to sway such insensitive souls in their determination to perpetrate the portending massacre!

Rapid contact with BR at Stoke soon prompted a letter to Bill from Mr Dow, this effectively *promising* that BR would continue to honour its contract with the RCTS and that No 46256 would be retained from withdrawal for two further weeks, especially to work the train.

Ironically, this was a major coup, for, quite by chance, the Society had transpired to obtain the very last revenue-earning job of all for a 'Princess Coronation' in BR service. At the time, however, the majority of those who had purchased tickets would have been remained oblivious of this fact … some, possibly, not until they actually joined the train at its departure point.

Time passed by, and as the day that the remainder of the seventeen other working survivors were to be withdrawn had come and gone and 'Sir William' hadn't turned a wheel since its own last outing to

LEFT & RIGHT: The great day has dawned and at shortly after 9-00am on 26th September 1964, No 46256 'Sir William A Stanier FRS' awaits departure from its birthplace at Crewe, with the RCTS 'Scottish Lowlander' special, which it will work as far as Carlisle. Thanks to some considerable elbow-grease by shed staff during the previous few days, it positively gleams in the autumn light and the waiting multitude, to a man, must surely have felt it difficult to believe that this was destined to be its last day in service. Preston fireman Brian Fare clearly has his fire well prepared and is now taking a well-earned breather whilst he awaits the "off". Meanwhile, footplate inspector Ernie Allcock finds the time to chat with other railwaymen who have come along to pay their last respects. [Both Pictures: Bill Ashcroft]

Carlisle of over a week and a half previously to that, this must have created some anxious moments. However, in order to ensure that it remained in full working order, 46256 then came to be rostered for a few more workings, the first of which found it at Polmadie shed on 14th September – having presumably arrived there on an overnight sleeper duty. Finding its way in due course back to Crewe, on 1M46, the 19-00 Glasgow Central to London Marylebone – presumably as far as Crewe, 16th September saw it heading north again at the head of 1S53, the 09-25 Crewe-Perth and returning south as far as Carlisle that same evening with 3M04, the 18-44 Aberdeen-Manchester (Oldham Rd) fish. The very next afternoon, it continued on to home base with 4A11, the 16-11 Carlisle-Willesden fitted-freight. Those tasks accomplished, and with no concerns arising, all appeared well!

The following 9 days for No 46256 were spent inside Crewe North shed, being prepared for its final duty and what would now very definitely be the swansong of the class.

Saturday 26th September 1964 – the final 'Duchess' working takes place

The great day dawned and, at Crewe – the departure point of the 'Scottish Lowlander' – No 46256, in the capable hands of Preston driver George Lilley and fireman Brian Fare, slowly drew its train out from the carriage sidings and into Platform 3. It not having been the cleanest of Crewe North's stud for a while, thanks to some considerable elbow-grease by shed staff during the previous few days, its maroon paintwork positively gleamed in the autumn light and the waiting multitude, to a man, must surely have felt it difficult to believe that this was destined to be its last day in service.

The journey from Crewe to Preston, with an intermediate pick-up stop at Warrington, was on a relatively easy schedule and, with a full hour being allowed, it was no surprise that arrival at Preston was a couple of minutes early. A crowd of waiting passengers, including this writer and many friends, had been gathering for some time at the south end of Platform 5 and excitement had grown as, well over a mile distant on the down-fast line, the unmistakable profile of the very last of Stanier's express steam giants was seen to emerge from under Skew Bridge and to gradually approach over the lofty embankment across the Ribble Valley. Its polished boiler-top glinting in backlit sunlight, over the points and under the massive semaphore gantries 46256 clattered and, still at a fair pace, away on under the cavernous roof, taking its 12-coach load right to the far end of the lengthy platform.

Passengers awaiting the following service – the 09-25 Crewe to Aberdeen, which had departed Crewe a mere ten minutes after the special – arose from platform seats and started to walk across to the carriages now drawing to a halt … that was, until platform staff intervened to inform them that this was certainly *not* their train. An excusable mistake perhaps for, it cannot be denied that a 1X75 reporting number would mean precious little to 'Joe Public', but, on the other hand, quite coincidentally a mere 10 days earlier, the very same Aberdeen train had actually been worked by no other than No 46256!

All present being anxious to obtain photographs of such a historical moment, such was probably the reason why the Preston stop had to be extended to double that scheduled. The Aberdeen train being not all that far behind, once the stragglers had eventually been gathered up and hurriedly shepherded aboard, all were treated to acceleration in fine style up the bank out of the platform and we were soon bowling along, reaching 74mph by Brock water troughs on the Lancaster 'racing stretch'.

Bill, possessing a footplate pass on this stage, to accompany Preston driver Jack ('Jonty') Johnson and fireman Roy ('Chalky') White along with Inspector Ernie Allcock, recalled that there actually transpired to be a shortage of steam not long afterwards. He added that, until he had

MILES	LOCATION	SCHED. (MINS)	ACTUAL (MINS)	SPEED (MPH)
	Date: Saturday 26th September 1964			
	Log: 1X75 Preston to Carlisle			
	Loco: No 46256 'Sir William A Stanier FRS'			
	Load: 416 tons tare / 450 tons gross			
	Driver: Joe Johnson / **Fireman:** Roy White (both of Preston)			
0.0	PRESTON	0	0	0
9.5	Garstang & Catterall	13	11.47	74/70
	Signal check			
21.0	Lancaster Castle	23	23.05	20
24.9	Signal stop			0
27.3	Carnforth	28	32.04	55/62
34.5	Milnthorpe	35	39.04	72
40.1	Oxenholme	43	44.36	52/54
47.1	Grayrigg		53.29	42 (min)
50.5	Milepost 29½	Permanent-Way slack		25
53.1	Tebay	59	61.27	60
54.5	Tebay North IBS		62.49	61
56.1	Scout Green		64.38	48
58.7	Shap Summit	69	68.14	38 (min)
	Signal stops			0
90.1	CARLISLE	104	18.56	0

Net Journey Time: 90½ min

Log Courtesy: Mr HG Ellison

PREVIOUS PAGES - LEFT: *A spectacular vision, looking down that long red boiler from the fireman's seat, the home and distant signals are pulled-off for the down through line, avoiding the platform roads, as the 'Scottish Lowlander' approaches Lancaster Castle station. Commanding the skyline can be seen the structure from which the station took its name.*
[Picture: Bill Ashcroft]

PREVIOUS PAGES - RIGHT: *At the very peak of the climb to Grayrigg summit, 'Sir William A Stanier FRS' is travelling at 42mph with its 12-coach train as it passes through the long-abandoned platforms of the former Grayrigg Station (closed in 1954). Shap is yet to come, but, just round the corner, however, an as yet unannounced signal check awaits the special at the entry to the Lune Gorge. The final slog is not going to be an easy one. [Picture: Howard Malham]*

LEFT: *Producing a performance worthy of a Stanier 'Duchess' at its very best, the final ascent is made of Shap Fell ... the very last of a great pageant of magnificent machines that had transported millions between the English and Scottish capitals down the years. Having just passed the remote Scout Green 'box, No 46256 is travelling at 48mph and already well past the halfway point on the ascent to the summit with its unassisted 12-coach load.*
[Picture: Trevor Owen – Courtesy WH Ashcroft Collection]

ABOVE: *Upon arrival at Carlisle, the much-anticipated meet-up occurs between two celebrated 'rivals'. Was this for the first time ever, was the question on many lips? Whether so, or not, the occasion was certainly destined to be the last! Prepared for its own record-breaking run over the Waverley Route, No 60007 'Sir Nigel Gresley' waits quietly on the centre-roads, as No 46256 'Sir William A Stanier FRS' is uncoupled from 1X75 and, following which it will run to Upperby depot for servicing.*
[Picture: Dugald Cameron]

booked on duty, the young fireman appeared only to have been aware that he was to be 'second-man' on *"a relief to Edinburgh"* and had fully expected to have had his feet up by now, all the way to Carlisle on a Type 4 diesel! Indeed, just before he passed away a couple of years ago, Roy did share with a friend that he had arrived at work for this job immediately following a *"good Friday night out on the Boddington's"* in the nearby (but now long-vanished) Theatre Hotel on Fishergate in Preston ... a one-time regular watering-hole for footplate personnel - whether off, or *on*, duty! As Bill further added, on the day, despite Roy's undoubted sterling efforts, the unfortunate fellow soon appeared to be a bit out-of-practice, especially on Stanier Pacifics!

Fortuitously, a permanent-way slack and a signal-check occurred immediately before Lancaster, so in addition to some assistance from the driver and inspector, this soon helped to bring the boiler round and matters seemed to improve thereafter. A brief signal-stop before Carnforth, however, kept speed down on the approaches to the long slog at 1 in 106 to Grayrigg summit, which we passed at 42 mph, and then there followed another lengthy permanent-way slack just beyond Low Gill at the entry to the Lune Gorge.

PREVIOUS PAGES - LEFT: *Having come off the train, Preston driver Joe Johnson and footplate inspector Ernie Allcock appear to be as interested in the proceedings as are the several tour passengers anxious to obtain their last ever picture of a 'Coronation' in daylight. No 46256 'Sir William A Stanier FRS' runs forward towards Carlisle No 4 signal box, ready to retire to Upperby depot for servicing. [Picture: Ron Herbert]*

PREVIOUS PAGES - RIGHT: *A4 pacific No 60007 'Sir Nigel Gresley' backs down onto the waiting stock as 'Royal Scot' No 46128 'The Lovat Scouts' prepares to take out a following northbound departure. Some of the tour organisers may well have found the presence of the Stanier 7P to be somewhat ironic, given that this was one of the types of motive power that they had requested the Scottish Region to provide to work the special north of Carlisle and were refused "as there won't be any available by September"! [Picture: Peter Fitton]*

RIGHT: *Having been described by one passenger on the train as "running like an engine possessed", on the final leg of the over 8 gruelling miles uphill at 1 in 75 to Whitrope Summit, having passed through the isolated outpost of Riccarton Junction, No 60007 'Sir Nigel Gresley' winds around the lower slopes of White Knowe and Stitchell Hill on the reverse curves for which the Waverley Route was famous. Since closure of the line in 1969, this locality has been totally transformed and the bare and desolate moorland seen here is now covered with massive fir plantations. [Picture: Paul Riley]*

LEFT: *After its record-breaking ascent of the notorious climb to Whitrope Summit, A4 pacific No 60007 'Sir Nigel Gresley' takes on a much-needed replenishment of water at Hawick. The very cramped station site here was built on a sharp curve with wooden platforms extending onto the viaduct crossing the River Teviot. To the right of the locomotive can be seen the former NBR motive power depot. Everything seen in this picture disappeared in around 1975 and a leisure centre and car park now occupies the whole area. [Picture: Peter Fitton]*

A worthy performance by any account!

Undeterred, the crew rose to the occasion and put the loco hard at it over Dillicar troughs, through Tebay and on up Shap Fell. We passed Tebay at 60mph and speed actually increased to 61mph on the 1 in 146 by Tebay North intermediate block section signal. The technical experts aboard reckoned that such an effort had involved an estimated drawbar horsepower of 2,400 and No 46256 then came to drag the 450 ton train over the top of the final 1 in 75 past Shap Summit 'box in 6¾ minutes, at 38mph ... a performance worthy of a Stanier 'Duchess' at its very best.

The Meet-up of the 'Rivals'!

At Carlisle, the much anticipated loco-change took place, with 60007 taking 46256's place at the front end and, just for an all-too-brief moment, the two 'great men' were stood alongside each other on adjacent tracks!

Although quite unplanned, the leading vehicle of the train was also of former LNER parentage and this, somehow, seemed quite appropriate, given the imminent direction of travel. The train itself, however, was wrongly announced at Carlisle as the 09.30 Manchester – Glasgow and at least one intending Glasgow-bound passenger boarded here ... despite the 200 or so gricers seen to be piling off to take photos of the locos! (Maybe this sort of thing happened every day at Carlisle back in those distant times?!)

Two passed firemen from Kingmoor, Driver McLaren and Fireman Whiteman, were in charge of the A4 and obviously keen to impress! The tremendous run that followed was described thus by John F. Clay in the RCTS journal 'The Railway Observer':

The sensation of the day was still to come, however. No.46256 was very appropriately replaced by 60007 'Sir Nigel Gresley' and the train set off six minutes late and was promptly put on the wrong road at Carlisle No 3.

After setting back, we restarted, passing Canal Junction 12½ minutes late. There were gloomy forebodings on the train, as 450 tons was a heavy unaided load for the 'Waverley' route, and anyway, wasn't an A4 a flyer rather than a climber? We thought we could hardly hope for much recovery, but how wrong we were! 60007 ran like an engine possessed and was 7½ minutes early at Niddrie Junction, after a ten-minute stop at Hawick.

"A recorder travelling alone could hardly expect others to accept a net time of 58½ minutes from Carlisle to Hawick, and 15 min 14 sec. from Newcastleton to Whitrope Sidings and it was just as well that this was a rail tour with many confirmatory timings. It is safe to assume that the equivalent drawbar horse power was in the 2,000 to 2,100 range and that effort was sustained for 15 minutes! This would appear to be the highest power output ever recorded by an A4 in this particular speed range and it is as great a tribute to the designer's masterpiece as this same engine's many high-speed exploits. In the whole history of steam railroading, is there any other major incline where the heaviest published unaided load also made the fastest recorded ascent? Driver McLaren and Fireman Whiteman of Kingmoor are to be congratulated on proving that, even at the eleventh hour, it was possible to write another brilliant page in the history of steam."

		SCHED.	ACTUAL	SPEED
MILES	**LOCATION**	**(MINS)**	**(MINS)**	**(MPH)**
0.0	CARLISLE	0	0	0
	Carlisle No 3	stop and reverse (wrong road)		
1.4	Canal Jct 4	4	10.27	20
14.1	Riddings Jct	21	24.12	53
16.1	Milepost 82		26.58	40
24.2	Newcastleton	34	36.17	61
28.8	Steele Road		41.58	39
31.1	Milepost 67		45.50	36
32.1	Milepost 66		47.35	33
	(severe curves)			
32.4	Riccarton Jct	50	47.56	35
33.1	Milepost 65		49.20	34
34.1	Milepost 64		51.00	37
34.5	Whitrope Siding	55	51.31	38
38.3	Shankend		55.53	66 (max)
45.4	HAWICK	71	65.06	0

Date: Saturday 26th September 1964

Log: 1X75 Carlisle to Hawick

Loco: No 60007 'Sir Nigel Gresley'

Load: 416 tons tare / 450 tons gross

Driver: Maclaren / **Fireman:** Whiteman (both of Kingmore)

Net Journey Time: 58½ min

Approx. equivalent drawbar horsepower at milepost 67 = 2075

Log Courtesy: Mr HG Ellison

LEFT: Niddrie West Junction was the point at which the engine change from 60007 to 60009 took place. Located at the end of the spur connecting the Waverley Route to the Edinburgh Suburban Line (avoiding Waverley station), in this view, the direct route from Monktonhall Junction and the ECML is on the left and Newcraighall (Klondyke) Colliery stands in the background. [Picture: Peter Fitton]

RIGHT: To avoid the centre of Glasgow, No 60009 was routed via the City of Glasgow Union Railway Line. With the unmistakably typical Glasgow tenement blocks as a backcloth, here at St John's Junction, the locomotive was removed from the train to take water in an adjacent siding. Note the fireman encouraging the supply to run more freely, from a most precarious position – a process that would certainly be frowned upon today ... as would that of passengers being permitted to alight from a train straight onto running lines! [Picture: Peter Fitton]

(Indeed, so much for the earlier-expressed concerns of the ScR motive power department in recommending the best loco for the job!!)

Having already achieved two notable feats of steam haulage, we had arrived at Hawick before time. Water was taken here and then good running continued with an ascent to Falahill Summit that proved to be nearly as notable as the earlier effort. (There had been slightly faster climbs up the Gala Water, but never with such a load as this!)

Given that there now seemed to be less cinders raining down on the roofs of the train, the majority of the fireworks seemed to be over and so Bill and quite a few others made their way along to the restaurant car to partake in lunch. Debating whether to have the grill, or the salad – the options ultimately offered consisted of salad or salad (and there wasn't even much of that remaining!) After a chat with the chief conductor, it became clear that, in spite of the detailed pre-bookings, the Restaurant Car Department (later to become 'Travellers Fare', prior to privatisation) simply had not believed the figures for meals ordered and had sent out the vehicle stocked with insufficient supplies. With the

train catering staff at the brunt of abuse as a result of the inadequacies of their superiors, pleading phone calls to Edinburgh from Hawick had produced no joy as no-one could be found to re-stock a restaurant car on a Saturday afternoon – not even in Scotland's capital city!

The RCTS stewards, therefore, did a quick public relations job through the train and made contact in the process with a native of Edinburgh who knew the Niddrie district intimately – our next booked stop. This gentleman took Bill on one side for a few quiet words, immediately following which, once we had come to a halt, accompanied by a handful of stewards and the restaurant-car staff, he set off across the wastes of the old yard area, through the fence and straight into a nearby grocer's shop!

The expedition returned shortly afterwards, adequately laden with loaves, butter, trays of eggs, bacon, ham, and sausages, having virtually cleared the shop out of quick-cook food. We were back in business! However, in the absence of today's public address systems, another lengthy trip through the train was then needed to advise the 'starving masses'!

Not one Gresley pacific ... but two!

In the meantime, 'Sir Nigel' and our young Kingmoor crew had given way to 'Union of South Africa' for the run back to Carlisle via Glasgow. Having negotiated the Edinburgh suburban line at a moderate pace, a special stop was made en-route at Lenzie Junction to set down the passenger who had joined at Carlisle in mistake for the train behind us and it was to be hoped that, despite the slight delay in his arrival home, he had enjoyed being present when history was being made!

Omens of the sort of problems that occasionally plague present-day steam-tours were experienced at Glasgow St Johns, when the loco uncoupled and ran off into a siding next to a water column to replenish its supply. The antiquated water-tank was clearly incapable of disgorging its contents in such a rapid manner and the fireman was forced to ascend a steep and treacherous ladder in order to provide further encouragement. At this stage, there was also a problem with the steam-heat connection between locomotive and train, which caused further delay, both here and later at Carlisle. We departed 16 minutes late and ran along the avoiding lines to the south of the city centre to join the old Glasgow & South Western main line. Making a good climb through the Barrhead Gap with a minimum of 29 mph. we had recovered three minutes by the Kilmarnock stop and good running after this helped us recover more time all the way to Carlisle.

As JF Clay continued, *"An excellent start to Mauchline followed, and although the engine seemed to be eased slightly on the upper part of the climb, New Cumnock was 26 minutes 12 seconds, now only eight down. It is doubtful if any modern engine has ever been allowed to run downhill with the abandon of Johnnie McIntosh who, with his Manson 4-6-0, once did the 86.9 miles from New Cumnock to Dumfries in thirty minutes. Our driver kept carefully within the Scottish Region's overall 75 mph limit. He opened out on the ascent of Ironhirst Bank, where speed was sustained up the 1 in 150 at almost 60 mph. With a final net time of ninety-six minutes for the 91.2 miles Kilmarnock to Carlisle, 60009 had no cause for shame, and engine and crew departed from the train to a well-earned cheer."*

LEFT: Having already enjoyed some high-speed running along the former Glasgow & South Western main line, in the late afternoon sunshine, No 60009 'Union of South Africa' takes on a much-needed tender-full of water at Kilmarnock, before completing the final leg of its journey non-stop via Dumfries into Carlisle. Today, much of this route is reduced to single-track. [Picture: Peter Fitton]

RIGHT: No 46256 "Sir William A Stanier FRS" is serviced at Carlisle Upperby motive power depot before commencing its last ever journey of all. Its sparkling external condition belies the inescapable fact that, upon its return to Crewe North shed, it would never turn another wheel in steam again. [Picture: Ron Herbert]

Moreover, as a further aside, reverting back to the RCTS's original request for locos and the Scottish Region's subsequent somewhat negative response, it must be observed that, on the way north, we had passed No 60083 'Sir Hugo', an A3 pacific in visibly less than perfect condition at Millerhill yard on a freight from Carlisle - which it had worked ahead of us over the Waverley route. If that was not enough, in Kingmoor shed yard on the return, we then saw a re-built 'Patriot' in steam and, as was later to be discovered, yet more of the same types were inside the shed at the time. How different might that day have been, had we not had those two superb A4s to rely upon?

Last-ever Stanier pacific journey commences

At Carlisle Citadel station, in the approaching dusk 46256 reversed back onto the stock and with 60009 pausing alongside on one of the middle roads - perhaps in final salute to a much-revered rival - seemed fully prepared to assume its place in the history books to head what we all were seriously acknowledging was going to be the very last-ever run over Shap of a Stanier pacific.

Rain was starting to fall and, following a cold start some 12 mins behind booked time, pace was somewhat pedestrian until the engine warmed through. A very tolerable net time of 38¾ minutes was nonetheless achieved by the Upperby crew for the 31½ miles up to Shap Summit and, with a 450 ton train; this effort was comparable with the best efforts of the 'Duchesses' ten years previously. Five minutes had already been recovered at this point and with falling grades ahead, a punctual arrival at Preston and Crewe seemed probable.

The noise through the many open windows was superb and, storming through Lancaster Castle station in the darkness on the fast line, waiting passengers for a late evening electric service to Green Ayre and Morecambe just stared in awe. Preston was all too soon reached; doors

were opening everywhere and, at the end of Platform 6, 'Sir William' became immediately surrounded by passengers – all anxious to soak-in the atmosphere, if not also to obtain that final photograph. The 3 minutes booked stop became extended to 6 and it is perhaps better to say little of the series of operating mishaps that had already put us 15 minutes late by this point and, of which, much more was to come.

With Preston driver George Williams and fireman Keith Hilton (the *third* crewing by Preston men during this memorable day!) now at the controls, all too soon whistles were blowing; those continuing onwards to Crewe were hurriedly clambering back on board and with the starting signal showing an impatient green, slowly the long train started to move forward. Gathering pace, carriages ever more rapidly flashed past, with faces peering from every droplight window. This was the last time ever … we watched it happen in silence and all too soon it was all over.

Continuing onwards onto the up-fast line, the red tail-lamp disappeared into the night… the very last of a great pageant of magnificent machines that had transported many millions between the English and Scottish capitals down the years. Those at the platform end gazed in silence as a flickering halo of yellow light, illuminating the engine's exhaust, rapidly receded into the distance and on up the 1 in 100 past Skew Bridge 'box. Many lingered for a while, quite unable to contain their emotions. That was it! We had just said farewell to the 'Duchesses' – for ever … or so we then thought!

A halt had to be made at Wigan (North Western), as the aforementioned tail lamp seemed to have extinguished itself … perhaps in an act of final defeat and then, due to Moore troughs being out of action, with the tender water-level already causing concern, an enforced stop had to be made for replenishment at Warrington (Bank Quay) and this resulted in the final arrival at Crewe being 40 mins after booked time. Nevertheless, with all the other mixed feelings prevalent at that very moment amongst the assemble multitude as No 46256 went onto North shed for its final disposal, timekeeping was probably the last thought entering anyone's mind. 'Sir William A Stanier FRS' was never to turn a wheel again in steam.

As a further postscript to the day, and so the story went, during the return journey discussions had been taking place with regard to organising a 'whip-round' to preserve this such superb specimen of its breed. Evidently, enquiries that were made are reputed to have been met with an official response quoting a price for No 46256 of £2,400 'as

LEFT: **Having just traversed the Glasgow & South Western main line, the 'Scottish Lowlander' arrives back at Carlisle behind Gresley A4 pacific No 60009 'Union of South Africa' and which, in the gathering dusk, is about to hand over to No 46256 'Sir William A Stanier FRS'. The blower is on and the Upperby crew appear well-prepared to make their last-ever journey to Crewe behind a Stanier pacific. [Picture: Howard Malham]**

RIGHT: **"Nulli Secundus" [Picture: Alan Castle]**

it stood'. Sadly, many of us at that stage in our lives were either merely school-leavers, or had recently married and had young families. With few others possessing such huge amounts of cash at their disposal and certainly the 'Alan Peglers' of this world being still pitifully few and far between, there was nothing further that could be done. If that £2,400 had still been on offer today, who wouldn't have been the first to produce his cheque book?!

Bill, a life-long lover of Stanier express-power, himself retrospectively summed it all up, *"Other people have their own thoughts about memorable railtours, but the 'Scottish Lowlander' was my nadir."* Notwithstanding such a poignant statement, writing of the tour in the 'Railway Observer' shortly afterwards, J F Clay observed, *"It will have to be recorded that operating efficiency has rarely matched the proven capacity of these great engines!"* He did then add … and with some justification, *"Steam enthusiasts, who in their general philosophy accept the transitory nature of all good things, should waste no time on vain regrets because of the massacre of the 'Duchesses' …. at least they have been spared the ignominious 'living death' of the Annesley 'Scots'".*

Someone who once referred 'tongue-in-cheek' to the invariably rough-riding Austerity 2-8-0s as *"Canklow Scots"* was a person who had clearly also experienced at first-hand the deliberate run-down of the Great

Central main-line and its already generally 'clapped-out' motive power that had been cascaded onto the few surviving services. We had to be grateful that, at the very least, the 'Princess Coronations' of the West Coast main-line were permitted to meet their demise with some dignity!

Fifty years to the fore … nostalgia reigns supreme

Nostalgia, the stuff that stirs the imagination … of memories from a gentler, more innocent age and, within its spell, the romance created by the last giants of steam will ever endure - does possess advantages. It gives us an opportunity to draw upon feelings that we were unable to express in our youth and, in now more mature years, there exists an ever-growing yearning to re-visit past times, especially those that are recalled with so much affection.

Quite amazingly, thanks to the efforts of some remarkable people, precisely 50 years to the fore, that memorable journey of September 1964 came to be repeated utilising the same two types of locomotive and over as much of the same route as was still possible.

Sadly, though, No 46256 - the ultimate development of Stanier's 'magnum opus' and the subject of our undivided admiration during that unforgettable day now so long ago - was no more.

ABOVE: With wintry conditions somehow in keeping with the solemnity of the occasion, on 28th November 1964, No 46257 'City of Salford' commences its last ever ascent of Shap Fell. Seen departing from Tebay, dead within the consist of a freight headed by Newton Heath's No 44934, it is about join several of its sisters in store at Carlisle Upperby depot. The former Kingmoor engine's stay there was, however, only to be of brief duration, for it would not be long before 46257 was to head north again, over the Border and towards its ultimate and inevitable destiny in an Ayrshire scrapyard. [Picture: Maurice Burns]

The author wishes to acknowledge the invaluable assistance provided by the following gentlemen in the preparation of this book: Robert J Clarke, Mike Claxton, Chris Coates, Dugald Cameron, Robert Downham, Arthur Haymes, Ron Herbert and with special thanks being extended to Bill Ashcroft, Peter Fitton and Paul Wood